Catholic Bishops

A Memoir

Catholic Bishops

A Memoir

by

John Tracy Ellis

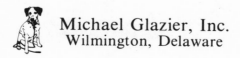

Michael Glazier, Inc.
Wilmington, Delaware

Acknowledgments

The publisher wishes to thank the following for use of illustrations: *The New World* and *The Chicago Catholic* (New World Photos) (p. 18 and p. 21); *The Monitor*, San Francisco (p. 42); Archives of the Archdiocese of Baltimore (p. 49 and p. 139); *The Pittsburgh Catholic* (p. 125); *The Boston Pilot*, Boston (p. 71 and p. 117); *The Catholic Standard and Times*, Philadelphia (p. 103); *New York Catholic* (p. 82 and p. 92); Religious News Service (p. 98).

First paperback edition November 1984

First hardcover edition published in January 1984 by Michael Glazier, Inc., 1723 Delaware Avenue, Wilmington, Delaware 19806 • © 1984 by John Tracy Ellis. All rights reserved • Library of Congress Card Catalog Number: 83-82626 • International Standard Book Numbers: 0-89453-371-1, hardcover; 0-89453-463-7, paper • Typography by Joyce Cartagena • Cover design by Brother Placid, O.S.B. • Printed in the United States of America.

In Loving Memory
of
John M. McNamara (1878-1960)
Auxiliary Bishop of Washington

Contents

A Prefatory Note

Every attempt at autobiography must necessarily be incomplete, since one cannot tell the whole story, and that for many reasons among which a lack of remembrance is often a prime factor, along with the practice of selection. In that regard Cardinal John Heenan, Archbishop of Westminster, was probably more forthright than most when in 1971 he entitled a volume of his memoirs, *Not the Whole Truth*. If such be the case with autobiographies in general, *a fortiori* it is true when a single aspect or theme of one's memories is singled out as in the present work.

Yet even fragments of knowledge can be instructive, provided they deal with real life in a spirit inspired by a desire to recreate a portion of one's past with fidelity and sincerity. The effort to recall certain characteristics of Catholic bishops whom I have known over the last half century will, therefore, I hope, be of interest either to those who may have known one or more of these churchmen, or to those who may wish to gain further information about bishops whose names figure prominently in the American Catholic story during the years since 1930.

While I would not subscribe *in toto* to the judgment of Humphrey Carpenter, author of books on W. H. Auden and J. R. R. Tolkien, I confess there is enough plausibility in it to make the writer of memoirs take pause. Carpenter stated:

> Autobiography is probably the most respectable form of lying. No one expects the whole truth in any case, how could it be revealed, since the person we know least is likely to be ourself? The worst autobiographies are those that fail to take account of the deceptive nature of the genre; the best are those that exploit it.[1]

If I am free from the consciousness of having lied in this autobiographical effort, I do not pretend that I have entirely escaped the subtle influence of self-deception about persons and events now far distant in time, nor do I discount the fact that the twilight years have a tendency to increase one's doubts about how well one really knows one's own self.

In the opening sentence of the memoirs of Nicholas Murray Butler, long President of Columbia University, he declared:

> One who has had and is having the inestimable pleasure and satisfaction of a busy, an interesting and a happy life, and who has enjoyed and is enjoying worldwide contacts and associations of the greatest possible charm and importance, may easily overestimate the value to others of even an imperfect record of those things which he has seen and heard.[2]

If I can claim a measure of the 'pleasure and satisfaction of a busy, an interesting and a happy life,' I must disclaim any such important and worldwide contacts as those enjoyed by Dr. Butler. My life has been lived on a very much lower level than that of Columbia's famous president, and that is why I

---

[1] *New York Times Book Review*, Sunday, February 7, 1982, p. 9.

[2] Nicholas Murray Butler, *Across the Busy Years. Recollections and Reflections.* New York: Charles Scribner's Sons. 1935. p. 1.

have more than once questioned if I may not, indeed, be overestimating the value to others of this 'imperfect record.'

> In thus employing myself I shall yield to the inclination so natural to old men of talking of themselves and their own actions, and I shall indulge it, without being tiresome to those who, from respect to my age, might conceive themselves obliged to listen to me, since they will be always free to read me or not.[3]

These words of Benjamin Franklin written to his son in 1771 tell something of my frame of mind in attempting this memoir. In recent years I have been urged more than once to undertake such a work. In fact, nearly a decade ago I wrote seven chapters of my memoirs, but due to several rejections by prospective publishers, the distraction of other duties, and a loss of interest I abandoned the idea. If this renewed effort on a more limited scale should be found of any value by those 'free to read me or not,' I shall be content. In any case, I trust that my memory will support my desire to tell the truth as I recall it, mindful of the reservation of Johnson's famous biographer, James Boswell, who once remarked to Sir Joshua Reynolds, "though I tell nothing but the truth, I have still kept in my mind that the whole truth is not always to be exposed."[4] In that regard, I suspect, it is the rare person, indeed, who could bear with telling literally the 'whole truth' about his or her life. Let this suffice for an introductory note.

•

Even a modest work of this kind leaves an author indebted to others. For reading the manuscript and offering helpful criticisms and suggestions I am indebted to three friends to whom I wish to express my appreciation, namely,

---

[3]Max Ferrand (Ed.), *The Autobiography of Benjamin Franklin.* Berkeley: University of California Press. 1949. p. 3.

[4]James Boswell, *The Life of Samuel Johnson.* Abridged by Edmund Fuller. New York: Dell Publishing Company. 1960. p. 9.

Monsignor Thomas M. Duffy, pastor of Blessed Sacrament Parish, Washington, Monsignor George G. Higgins, adjunct lecturer in theology, the Catholic University of America, and the Reverend Roland E. Murphy, O. Carm., George Washington Ivey Professor of Biblical Studies at Duke University. I wish also to express my gratitude to the staff of the Mullen Library of the Catholic University of America for their generous response to my repeated calls for assistance. Finally, may this memoir measure up in some degree to what Saint Thomas More had in mind when he expressed the wish, "that all such as will write may have the grace to write well, or at the least with none other purpose than to mean well...."

John Tracy Ellis
October 13, 1983

Bishops in Illinois

The first bishop on whom I laid eyes was Edmund M. Dunne, Bishop of Peoria, when in May, 1916, he came to old Saint Patrick's Church in Seneca, Illinois, to confirm us. I can still remember this burly churchman with the mitre tilting on an angle off his head and his cope veering off the opposite shoulder. This successor of the learned John Lancaster Spalding was known for his sharp intelligence, linguistic ability, and rather gruff manner. I was told years after that he endeared himself to his priests by declining the cathedraticum to which he was entitled since he was well enough off not to need the money. Although I never knew Bishop Dunne, I saw him from time to time, e.g., on visits to Saint Viator College in the years (1921-1927) when I was a student there. It was a small country school founded in 1865 that comprised at one time a boarding academy, a college, and a seminary, located in Bourbonnais, Illinois, then in the Archdiocese of Chicago. It enrolled a number of students who later made their mark, especially among the clergy of the Middle West, before it closed in 1938. The fame of one, Fulton J. Sheen, of course, went far beyond his native

Illinois, and that was true to a lesser degree of others, among them Gerald T. Bergan, second Archbishop of Omaha.

It was only after I began the study and teaching of American Catholic history in 1941 that I learned more about Bishop Dunne. When James E. Quigley, Archbishop of Chicago, died in 1915 the two leading candidates to succeed him were Dunne and Peter J. Muldoon, Bishop of Rockford, both of whom had numerous supporters among Chicagoans. The two Illinois bishops lost out, however, when in December, 1915, it was announced that George W. Mundelein, Auxiliary Bishop of Brooklyn, had been chosen. Among the Muldoon supporters was John J. Dennison, later pastor of Saint Mary of the Lake Church in Chicago. In my early priesthood I often stayed at his rectory with my lifelong friend, Edward V. Cardinal, C.S.V., who was in residence there during the years he taught history at Loyola University.

On one of those visits Monsignor Dennison told me that at the time of the Mundelein appointment he was in Washington visiting his classmate, William T. Russell, who died as Bishop of Charleston. He said that Russell informed him that the Apostolic Delegate, Archbishop Giovanni Bonzano, was coming to dinner. Upon the latter's arrival he was introduced to Dennison, and hearing he was from Chicago he stated, "You have a new archbishop." Dennison asked who it was, and the delegate replied, "His name begins with M and ends with N," whereupon the Chicagoan exclaimed, "Thank God, Muldoon!" only to have Bonzano state, "Oh, no, Mundelein." John Dennison confessed to me his keen disappointment and remarked that he scarcely knew who Mundelein was.

If the Muldoon party was disappointed, so were those who had backed Edmund Dunne. Their disappointment gradually faded, however, and by the time of Mundelein's installation (February, 1916), they had generally become reconciled to the stranger from New York. If the luncheon following the installation ceremonies was long remembered for an anarchist having poisoned the soup which left hundreds of the guests ill for hours thereafter, the occasion was also memorable for the manner in which the toastmaster, the same Dunne of Peoria, performed the task of introducing the new archbishop. Standing between Mundelein seated on one side and Bonzano on the other, he began with the formula customary in those days, "George William Mundelein, by the grace of God, and the favor of the Apostolic (pausing to bow toward the delegate) See, Archbishop of Chicago." The significance of the pause and the bow in the delegate's direction were, needless to say, caught at once by the largely clerical gathering, for it had meanwhile become known that it was the Roman friendship of earlier years between Bonzano and Mundelein that had brought about the latter's appointment. If Dunne enjoyed the mischievous scene—as did many of the churchmen in attendance—Bonzano was not amused; in fact, it was rumored that he was so incensed that he demanded an apology from the Bishop of Peoria. I never heard that he received it.

At the age of fifteen I was blissfully unaware, needless to say, of these happenings. A few years later, however, Mundelein came to be more than a name to me when in March, 1924, he was made a cardinal. Saint Viator, like all archdiocesan institutions, took pride in the honor paid to their archbishop. The event occasioned my early published literary effort when in the spring of 1924 *The Viatorian*, the school journal, carried an essay that I had been asked to write on the new cardinal.[5] I was nineteen at the time, and though I never knew Mundelein personally, I remember the stir caused by his visit to the college which afforded me my

---

[5]"Our Cardinal," *The Viatorian*, 41 (April, 1924), 4-9. I confess that a recent rereading of this youthful effort made me wince more than once. Its gross exaggerations and overdrawn literary flourishes would cause it to be dismissed today as woeful 'triumphalism.'

first glimpse of a Prince of the Church. As it turned out his twenty-three year tenure of the see gave Chicago its most progressive administration before his sudden death in October, 1939. In that sense the words he spoke at the reception in his honor on his return from Rome as a cardinal proved rather prophetic. Having outlined his plans for the years ahead, he remarked:

> This work will last and keep known to men my name long after the scarlet robes I wear have moulded in the tomb, and the red hat of the Cardinal swung high in the vaulted heights of my Cathedral.[6]

In 1927 I began graduate studies at the Catholic University of America, and I saw Cardinal Mundelein there a number of times, since the hierarchy then held their annual meeting on the campus. One such occasion had more significance than I then realized. It was November, 1928, and the university was to inaugurate its fifth rector, James Hugh Ryan, in the presence of President and Mrs. Calvin Coolidge. Shortly after noon I was returning from class when the hierarchy were assembled in front of Mullen Library to have their picture taken. There in the front row were the four American cardinals: O'Connell of Boston, Dougherty of Philadelphia, Hayes of New York, and Mundelein of Chicago. That afternoon at the inauguration ceremony virtually the entire hierarchy was present, but Mundelein was missing.

Many years later the university's chancellor, Michael J. Curley, Archbishop of Baltimore, with whom I became good friends while researching the life of his predecessor, Cardinal Gibbons, told me what had happened on the

---

[6]Quoted in Charles Shanabruch, *Chicago's Catholics: The Evolution of An American Identity.* Notre Dame: University of Notre Dame Press. 1981. p. 225. For Mundelein's signal achievements see Edward R. Kantowicz, *Corporation Sole. Cardinal Mundelein and Chicago Catholicism.* Notre Dame: University of Notre Dame Press. 1983.

morning of that November day. At the meeting of the university's Board of Trustees Mundelein had proposed that the university be closed in Washington and moved to Chicago. The proposal failed to win the trustees' approval, and Curley told me, "It was the Cardinal of Philadelphia who saved it." Parenthetically, I recall vividly the deep impression made on this unsophisticated graduate student by the address of the senior cardinal, William O'Connell. His diction was lofty and his rich metallic voice compelled attention. Frankly, I was spellbound, and I can still hear him as he turned to Coolidge and said, "Well do I remember the time, Mr. President, when you were the Lieutenant Governor of the Commonwealth of Massachusetts and I a humble Christian bishop." The implication was not lost even on the young graduate student from Seneca, Illinois!

Mundelein's new seminary of Saint Mary of the Lake had at the time been in operation for seven years, and it was his intention to make that the school of theology of the proposed university that would absorb as well, I believe, Loyola and De Paul Universities. His vision was broad and bold, to say the least, but this particular dream proved beyond even Mundelein's acknowledged ability to think and act in a big way. His was a mood that fitted Chicago admirably, for the metropolis of the Middle West had long been famous for 'thinking big.' It reminds me of a story that circulated at the time of the International Eucharistic Congress in Chicago in June, 1926. If the tale was apocryphal it was all the same typical of Chicago's spirit. A foreign churchman, dazzled by the spectacular events of the congress, was said to have exclaimed to a Chicagoan how stupendous it had all been. The latter accepted the compliment calmly, agreed the congress had been a success, but replied that this was nothing to what was coming. "What could outshine the congress?" asked the foreign visitor, to which the Chicagoan replied, "Cardinal Mundelein is making arrangements to hold the last judgment in Chicago."

As a junior in college I was at the congress and was duly impressed by the 100,000 men on Holy Name Night in Soldiers' Field, each with a lighted candle in hand, and I stood only a few feet from Mundelein and his eleven cardinal guests as they filed out of the stadium. Nor will I ever forget the thorough drenching I shared with thousands of others on the closing day at Mundelein, Illinois, when the heavens opened as the great procession was about halfway around the artificial lake. Only the papal legate under his canopy was spared, the same Giovanni Bonzano by then a cardinal in curia. Cardinal O'Connell who, let us say, did not share the same philosophy of life as his Chicago host, was alleged to have exploded as the procession finished its agonizing course at the seminary chapel. "Look at me," roared the man from Boston, "my silks are ruined. The vain man!" I had no 'silks,' but my college classmate, Tom Dunn, and I felt equally ruined as we slowly made our way back to the city late that afternoon.

Cardinal Mundelein

It was during my student days that I came gradually to understand who and what bishops were. True, my contacts with them were extremely limited, serving in some minor capacity or other when they visited the college or later the university. It was in that superficial way that I came to know something about the two handsome churchmen, Peter Muldoon of Rockford and Edward F. Hoban, Auxiliary Bishop of Chicago, as well as Bernard J. Sheil, a later Chicago auxiliary and a favorite alumnus of Saint Viator. It was Hoban who presided at commencement in June, 1927, when I received my bachelor's degree. Little did I then contemplate what an influential figure he was destined to become through his friendship with Amleto Giovanni Cicognani, Apostolic Delegate to the United States. The summer villa of Chicago's seminarians at Clearwater, Wisconsin, with Hoban as his host, afforded the delegate a comfortable spot where he could escape from the heat and humidity of Washington. As Bishop of Cleveland, Hoban was either directly responsible for a number of bishops or influential in starting them on their way, e.g., Floyd Begin to Oakland, Paul Hallinan to Charleston and then Atlanta, John Krol to Philadelphia, John Tracey to LaCrosse, and John Whealon as auxiliary in Cleveland before his promotion to Erie and subsequently to Hartford.

With Mundelein in Chicago the promising career of Peter Muldoon was cast into the shadows. I recall my late friend, Father Joseph P. Christopher, telling me that when word reached Muldoon that he was being named to Los Angeles in succession to Thomas J. Conaty who had died in September, 1915, he asked Christopher, then a priest of his diocese, to go to Highland Falls, New York, to make known to Monsignor Cornelius O'Keeffe, a close friend of Cardinal Pietro Gasparri, Secretary of State to Pope Benedict XV, his strong objection to being changed. Muldoon had the idea that Mundelein was behind the proposed move. In any case, his mind was conveyed to Rome and he escaped the 'exile.' After a delay of two years Los Angeles received John J. Cantwell in September, 1917. Muldoon was one of the most outstanding American bishops of the period, and he left a definite imprint on his age as chairman of the committee that brought into existence the National Catholic War Council (1917) and two years later its successor, the National Catholic Welfare Council (Conference), to say nothing of other notable services before his death at Rockford in 1927.

In Bourbonnais we saw more of Bernard Sheil—Benny as he was familiarly called—than any other bishop, for he came frequently and mixed rather freely with both faculty and students. That he had been a stellar baseball player did not diminish his stature, to be sure, and later when he won the favor of Mundelein who named him chancellor and auxiliary bishop, Viator men were proud. I came to know him fairly well by reason of my friendship with Ed Cardinal whom he named Director of the Sheil School of Social Studies, an adult education center which was an offshoot of the C.Y.O., Sheil's major enterprise. The bishop was prominently identified with liberal causes and was *persona grata* to numerous Protestants and Jews. Yet this man of pronounced liberal views in the public domain was known for his authoritarian manner in private life. He found it difficult to tolerate differences of opinion on the part of subordinates, and more than one in his service was summarily dismissed for their failure to conform.

Early in Sheil's episcopacy he won the admiration of President Franklin D. Roosevelt who in 1939 was anxious that he should succeed Mundelein as Archbishop of Chicago. Having failed in that objective, Roosevelt made known his desire that Sheil should become the first resident Archbishop of Washington. Given Sheil's liberal stances and his outspoken position on controversial issues such as Senator Joseph McCarthy whom he later vigorously opposed, he probably had little chance for either post with the cautiously conservative policies of Pope Pius XII and the Roman Curia in matters of this kind. Moreover, the knowledge that the White House was interested in these appointments would in all likelihood have frightened off the Holy See which is perennially sensitive to state interference in the naming of bishops. As time went on Roosevelt parted company from most of the Catholic prelates he had once favored, so that by the time of his death in 1945 his relations with Pius XII, Francis J. Spellman, Archbishop of New York, *et. al.*, were hardly more than correct. The warmth of the 1930's had turned almost to a chill as World War II drew to a close.

In the meantime Sheil's personal relations with Mundelein had likewise cooled, and at the celebration of his silver jubilee as a priest (1935), the cardinal presided at the Mass in Holy Name Cathedral, but contrary to his usual custom, remained silent. During the regime of Mundelein's successor, Samuel Stritch, Sheil was named an assistant at the

Bishop Bernard J. Sheil

pontifical throne and a titular archbishop, honorific titles
that carried no real power. In fact, the C.Y.O. had come
upon financial troubles that caused Cardinal Stritch grave
concern, and Monsignor J. Gerald Kealy, one of the Chicago consultors at the time, described for me a tense morning when word reached Stritch that Sheil was about to hold
a news conference at the C.Y.O. headquarters. The cardinal
hurried out of the consultors' meeting and drove
downtown—entering the C.Y.O. building for the first
time—'captured' the news conference and succeeded in
bringing off the delicate situation in a not unagreeable
fashion. With the advent of John P. Cody as Archbishop of
Chicago in 1965, Sheil was forced to retire. He moved to
Arizona where he died in 1969.

If I have determined to say nothing about living churchmen in this memoir, I trust that by the same token there will
not be too stark a violation of the old axiom, *de mortuis
nihil nisi bonum.* I would be less than honest were I to
pretend that this axiom has been observed to the letter in
what I write, but I have at least made a conscientious effort
to maintain its spirit.

At this point some biographical data are necessary to
provide the *mise en scène* for what is to follow. It was only
after my entrance to the university in 1927 that I came to
know a number of bishops rather well. Having received my
doctorate in history (1930), I taught for four years in the
Middle West and then returned to Washington in September, 1934, to begin theology in what was then called the
Sulpician Seminary (since 1940, Theological College of the
Catholic University of America). In the fall of 1935 I began
teaching a single undergraduate course in the university
which continued until my ordination (1938) when I was
appointed a full time instructor in the Department of History. In due time I was promoted to the various ranks and
remained until 1963 when I left for what turned out to be a
thirteen-year interval in San Francisco. During the 1930's I

taught during the summers in two of the university's branch summer sessions—in San Rafael, California (1933-1934) and in San Antonio, Texas (1935-1937), and in both places I became acquainted with bishops who had hitherto been no more than names to me.

2

University Rectors

At the time that I entered the university the total enrollment was under 900 students. Its small size enabled its rector—the title was changed to president in 1969—to preside after the fashion of a *pater familias*, and that is exactly what Thomas J. Shahan did. Of the nine bishops who headed the institution between 1889 and 1969 Shahan was undoubtedly the most learned, having done graduate work in church history in the Universities of Berlin and Paris after his ordination to the priesthood. He was named rector in 1909 and had the longest tenure of any, presiding over the university until 1928. I recall my first contact with the bishop when I was asked to serve as an assistant to my friend, Father Charles A. Hart, proctor of Saint John's Hall, a residence for undergraduates. That even minor matters of this kind passed through Shahan's hands was evident when he sent to interview me before he approved the appointment. By that time he was almost stone deaf, and I had to communicate by shouting through a long tube which he handed to visitors.

Now and then Bishop Shahan would be invited to address the seminar of Peter Guilday in which I was enrolled. He would lecture in a scholarly manner on some medieval topic such as the Abbey of Bobbio, and though his delivery was somewhat halting the substance was always solid and well prepared. Shahan's regime was relatively tranquil once he had cleared the air, so to speak, by bringing about the dismissal in 1910 of the Dutch-born Old Testament professor, Henry Poels, whose guilt was due to his having questioned the Mosaic authorship of the Pentateuch! It was a time of severe tension in Catholic intellectual circles following the stir over the so-called heresy of Americanism followed soon thereafter by the anti-modernist witchhunt subsequent to Pius X's encyclical, *Pascendi Dominici gregis* (September, 1907). If it was understandable that responsible officers in Catholic institutions should have been uneasy, it was, nonetheless, a grave injustice to Poels, an altogether admirable priest, a fact of which I became aware when I researched and wrote on the university's history. It was Shahan's contention that the university's reputation had been previously questioned by the views of several of the faculty, and he maintained that the institution could not afford to harbor anyone who was under suspicion at Rome. The Poels case reflected unhappily on an administration that otherwise made a creditable record.

Thomas Shahan was a strong man with decided opinions, and he did not easily brook opposition. Fulton Sheen once described for me an instance that illustrated that fact. Sheen had joined the theological faculty in 1926 and shortly thereafter Shahan proposed to them the introduction of undergraduates in the School of Theology. At a meeting which he called he asked each professor his opinion of the proposal. Sheen took the tube and made quite clear his opposition to introducing undergraduates into a school that had been limited to graduates since its inception nearly forty years before. Shahan was visibly displeased with the young professor's views, so Sheen remarked, and passed the tube on to Peter Guilday who told the rector what he wanted to hear.

The advent of James H. Ryan in 1928 ushered in one of

the most progressive and promising regimes in the university's history, a promise that was cut short in less than seven years through ecclesiastical obscurantism and intrigue. Ryan had a genuine academic sense and he was intent, as he was heard to say to his later sorrow, that he wished to make the university "a Catholic Harvard." He brought about a structural reorganization of the various schools that put the institution in line with that of the best universities in the land. Moreover, he constantly emphasized the need for high standards of scholarship and urged research and publication in all fields. My friend, Louis A. Arand, S.S., then in charge of the graduate priest students in Caldwell Hall, was close to Ryan. He told me that on his visits to the rector's suite he invariably found Ryan reading such things as the report of the president of Harvard to the Board of Overseers. In brief, Ryan took his position seriously and worked hard to equip himself as an enlightened administrator.

Unfortunately, James Ryan showed at times a rather

Bishop James H. Ryan, Rector of the Catholic University of America, President Franklin D. Roosevelt, and Mrs. Eleanor Roosevelt. The President received the honorary LL.D. degree at the 44th annual commencement of the University, June 14, 1933.

abrasive manner, and his abrupt speech and his aristocratic and aloof way of life made enemies. In his plan of reorganization, e.g., he decided without consulting the faculty to abolish the School of Philosophy and reduce it to a department within the arts and sciences graduate school and college. At a faculty meeting he was challenged for thus violating a directive of the Holy See by John J. Rolbiecki, whereupon Ryan promptly dismissed the philosopher. Rolbiecki carried the matter to Rome where he won his case and was reinstated with payment of all back salary. It was a humiliating defeat for the rector, but worse was to come.

At the time the Board of Trustees consisted in the main of the archbishops of the United States and a few selected bishops. Among their number was John T. McNicholas, O.P., Archbishop of Cincinnati, who had influence with the Apostolic Delegate, Archbishop Cicognani. McNicholas convinced Cicognani that Ryan was 'secularizing' the university, with the result that in August, 1935, it was announced that the university's rector had been named Bishop of Omaha. It was a severe blow that shook the confidence of many in the institution's future. Among those who resented the action was Archbishop Filippo Bernardini, first dean of the university's School of Canon Law, a friend of Ryan's, who had meanwhile been named Apostolic Delegate to Australia and then Nuncio to Switzerland. In the summer of 1950 I was in Switzerland and called on Bernardini in Bern. He asked about the university and volunteered his opposition to Ryan's removal. He declared, "It was a mistake and, in fact, Cicognani and I had a fight about it." The harm had been done, however, and once Rome had made the Omaha appointment nothing could be done to remedy the situation. Nor was it more than slender consolation to Ryan when the Diocese of Omaha was raised to metropolitan rank in August, 1945.

During my last years of graduate study I had a few brief meetings with Bishop Ryan, and I recall that shortly before I left Washington with the doctoral dissertation then in print he urged me to be sure to send copies of the book out to the learned journals for review. After I became editor of the *Catholic Historical Review* I would now and then ask him to review a book, and when Myron C. Taylor's *The Wartime Correspondence Between President Roosevelt and Pope Pius XII* appeared in 1947, Archbishop Ryan wrote a review and sent it in promptly. The proofs for the October issue were already underway, however, and I thought it would be time enough to publish it in the January, 1948, issue. During the bishops' annual meeting in November I encountered Archbishop Ryan in the corridor and went forward to greet him. But my greeting was met with a stormy countenance and he upbraided me in no uncertain terms for delaying the review. I tried to explain the circumstances, but he became so agitated and angry that I gave up and walked away. I remember how flushed his face became, but I had no idea at the time how unwell he was. Within a matter of two or three days he was dead, having suffered a heart attack upon his return to Omaha. I deeply regretted our final meeting, but it in no way lessened my admiration for one who had advanced the university in a notable way during his years as rector.

In an obituary which I wrote of the late archbishop for the *Review*, I summarized his university administration and remarked that upon his departure, "he willed to his successor a much strengthened institution." Unfortunately, the gains made under Ryan were somewhat dissipated with the arrival of Joseph M. Corrigan as sixth rector in 1936. The latter had been a director of retreats and Rector of Saint Charles Borromeo Seminary in Philadelphia, experiences that were vastly different from administering a university. This was only the latest instance of unenlightened interference from outside that told against the university, for it was the same Archbishop McNicholas who had unseated Ryan who was the principal promoter of Corrigan. The latter was a genuinely kind and good natured man of enormous girth whose wit helped initially to conceal the inadequacy of his preparation for the post.

On the day that the chancellor, Archbishop Curley, introduced him to the assembly faculty in familiar terms as "my old friend of thirty years ago," a summary of his previous career was given. Corrigan then rose, and while stating that all would agree that "a great deal of weight has gone into this appointment," he wheeled around on the dais to the amusement of many. I recall another occasion, much more formal in character, where Corrigan's sense of humor was not appreciated by some. It was the evening in 1942 when the university received its chapter of Phi Beta Kappa, thus becoming the second Catholic institution—the College of Saint Catherine was first—in the country to win the distinction. That year Phi Beta Kappa had its first woman president, Marjorie Hope Nicholson, Dean of Smith College and later professor of English at Columbia University. This genial, stout lady remarked that she conceived one of her principal duties was a defense of a liberal arts education. Not infrequently, she said, she was asked to differentiate between humanistic learning and practical education. She had just come from the University of Wyoming where she had installed a chapter of Phi Beta Kappa. While in Laramie she was informed that during the freshmen hazing week they got a cow into one of the women's dormitories, and no one seemed to know how to get the cow out. The president of the institution, a former cowboy, at last succeeded in lassoing the cow and bringing her down. This, said Miss Nicholson, was for her a demonstration of what constituted 'practical' education, whereupon she turned toward the rector and added, "I do not know how your rector would do lassoing a cow." With a twinkle in his eye Corrigan began his remarks by declaring, "The lady has taken considerable liberty with my size. I do not know how I would do lassoing a cow, but may I say that the lady herself has done a splendid job in throwing the bull"! I laughed heartily, as did many others, but there were those, such as my good friend and fellow historian, Leo F. Stock, who were not amused and who thought it was undignified to say the least.

Wit and geniality Joseph Corrigan had in ample measure but, alas, they were poor substitutes for academic learning and administrative efficiency where he was sadly at a loss. Not only did he rouse the ire of John A. Ryan, perhaps the most famous professor the university ever had, by his failure to recognize Ryan's rank as professor of moral theology rather than one who lectured on labor and economic issues, but his lack of acquaintance with the fundamentals of higher learning showed up as time went on. The point may be illustrated, I think, by the admission which Corrigan made to Louis Arand when he confessed that until he reached the campus he had not known that anyone could get a Ph.D. degree in any field but philosophy. The deterioration accelerated as grave disputes arose at the highest administrative level between Corrigan and Michael Curley, the chancellor. In the former's defense it should be said that he was not entirely a well man, a fact that was foreshadowed by his constant habit of falling asleep in public. I recall that when my friend, Charlie Hart, told me the rector fell asleep at breakfast I found it all but incredible; but one day at a university Mass in the National Shrine I had proof as I watched the bishop's mitre bob up and down as he struggled to fight off sleep while on the throne.

My personal relations with Bishop Corrigan, however, were entirely friendly. In the summer of 1941 he sent for be—at the suggestion, I later learned of Martin R. P. McGuire and Aloysius K. Ziegler—and asked if I would take the place of Monsignor Peter Guilday in teaching American Catholic history since Peter's diabetes had by then impaired his eyesight. Up to that time I had concentrated in European history and confessed that I knew next to nothing about the Catholic history of the United States.

"You can learn, can't you?" he asked. I said I could if given time, whereupon he replied, "We will give you time," I received a year's leave of absence at that point to prepare myself for the new field, spending half the year in Washington and the other half at Harvard where I audited courses in American social history and read widely in the rich sources of the Widener Library.

It was common knowledge that Joseph Corrigan was eager to be made a bishop, presuming, I suppose, that it was owed him in view of the tradition of his five predecessors. In any case, his desire was fulfilled when in April, 1940, he was named titular Bishop of Bilta, a title which somehow seemed fitting for this enormous man who thereafter was often referred to simply as 'Bilta.' He was an engaging speaker and preacher—when he was prepared—and his office brought him many invitations. It was after giving the commencement address at Loretta Heights College in Denver in June, 1942, that he contracted pneumonia on the train returning to Washington and died within a few days at the age of sixty-three.

It was the end of a troubled regime for the university. I remember being told by the Dean of the Graduate School that when Corrigan attended the annual meetings of the Association of American Universities he, the dean, was embarrassed by the fun which some of the secular educators poked at the rotund bishop. At a loss for ideas by which to set a creative course and to chart policy, Corrigan receded more and more from center stage and leaned on such people as the Italian-born Monsignor Francesco Lardone, professor of Roman law, and on directives from the Congregation of Seminaries and Universities as it was then called. As a consequence the academic progress along American lines made under Ryan was, as I have said, pretty much brought to a standstill.

I sincerely liked Bishop Corrigan as a person and felt sympathy for him. But his truly attractive qualities as a human being could not make up for the vacuities inherited from his narrow ecclesiastical training. It was only another sad example, to repeat, of how the university was made to suffer from the interference and bungling of churchmen who were ill equipped to foster true university education. In that connection I have more than once remarked that it has always been a mystery to me how Belgium's Catholic University of Louvain surmounted this type of influence and managed to maintain its status as an institution of world repute. I know no other explanation than the fact that the Belgian bishops since Louvain's reopening in 1834 have been for the most part university trained men. Parenthetically, for a century and a half all the primates of Belgium have been graduates of Louvain, men who understood and appreciated what a university was. In that regard Louvain's sister institution in Washington has been much less fortunate, and perhaps that alone seemed to justify the change to lay presidents in 1969.

Upon the death of Joseph Corrigan he was succeeded by Patrick J. McCormick who had been vice rector since 1936 and who was named a bishop in 1950. McCormick, a priest of the Diocese of Hartford, had come to the university in 1910 where for many years he taught the history of education. I knew this tall, handsome man rather well, although I doubt that any one knew him in a close and intimate way. He was reserved by nature, gentlemanly, soft spoken, and extraordinarily serene, a fact that prompted a clerical wag to say that his motto should be *semper paratus et numquam turbatus*. In any case, there was no doubt that the words fitted the man's demeanor and spirit in a peculiarly appropriate way. I often said that any one who thought to stir Patrick McCormick had only to gaze on that serene countenance to be convinced that the effort would prove futile.

My friend, Monsignor John K. Cartwright, Rector of Saint Matthew's Cathedral in Washington, once told me a story that illustrates the point. Cartwright had been invited to give the sermon at the annual Red Mass in the National Shrine, the arrangements for which were then in the hands of the university's School of Law. Invitations were sent to many distinguished figures of both Church and State, but by some oversight none was received by Patrick A. O'Boyle, Archbishop of Washington and chancellor of the university. The latter's annoyance soon became known, whereupon a card was hurriedly addressed to him which read 'admit two.' At that the chancellor's ire rose perceptibly. After the Mass McCormick asked Cartwright if he would remain for lunch. He accepted and went to the rector's suite in Curley Hall where he was served a cocktail. While they sipped their drinks McCormick quietly remarked, "I understand that the archbishop is disturbed over the arrangements for the Red Mass." Cartwright summarized for him what had happened, only to have his host calmly reply as he lifted his glass, "Well, those things will happen." The little episode epitomized the imperturbability with which he met practically every circumstance of life. If to some it was exasperating, it had a certain advantage in restoring a peaceful atmosphere to an institution tried by the turmoil of the previous regime.

Let me cite another example of this quality of Bishop McCormick which proved helpful to me personally. In my role as professor of American Catholic history I was ever on the *qui vive* for research topics for myself and my students that would make an original contribution to knowledge of the American Church's past. Virtually nothing had been done on the history of the university prior to my third book, *The Formative Years of the Catholic University of America* (1946). In the succeeding years I directed three master's theses which turned into book-size manuscripts on the administrations of the first three rectors, works published by the university press and authored by three of my priest graduate students, Patrick H. Ahern, Peter E. Hogan, S.S.J., and Colman J. Barry, O.S.B. These able young scholars were given full access to the unpublished sources, and as was inevitable, they turned up some rather seamy and unpleasant incidents in the internal struggles of the institution between its opening in 1889 and the end of the third rector's regime in 1909.

If the revelations of historic feuds and rivalries among American churchmen excite little wonderment or opposition in the 1980's, such was not the case in the 1940's. As the books on the university began to circulate there was heard in some quarters disapproval of the candor and openness with which they had been written. Meanwhile Patrick McCormick, in whose administration this work had been carried out, said nothing. One day I went to his office to inquire if I might examine a collection of letters of Thomas Bouquillon, the university's controversial first professor of moral theology, a collection which was in the rector's desk. Bishop McCormick readily admitted me to the documents, and when I finished my work I thanked him and started for the door. "By the way," he quietly remarked, "you know there has been some criticism of those books on the university." I confessed that I had heard there was. Nothing more was exchanged between us, I departed, and thereafter heard no more about it. Presumably, he was satisfied to dismiss the matter once he had called it to my attention. If it was not the exercise of leadership on a high level and in a significant context, it was, nonetheless, an admirable exercise of restraint of authority that left me and my students free to pursue our research and writing without the bedeviling interference from above that has ruined many a scholarly effort in ecclesiastical history. As the years have passed I have become increasingly grateful to Cardinal Newman for numerous striking statements on spiritual and intellectual themes. Among these I have always valued the following words spoken in a lecture of 1855 in Dublin:

> I say, then, that it is a matter of primary importance in the cultivation of those sciences, in which truth is discoverable by

the human intellect, that the investigator should be free, independent, unshackled in his movements; that he should be allowed and enabled, without impediment, to fix his mind intently, nay, exclusively, on his special object, without the risk of being distracted every other minute in the process and progress of his inquiry, by charges of temerariousness, or by warnings against extravagance and scandal.[7]

As humankind has attempted to grapple with the extraordinary complexities of life in the nuclear age there has been a mounting emphasis on leadership—or the lack of it—in every sector of human endeavor. Many will recall how *Time* magazine repeatedly stressed this subject during the 1970's with lengthy and elaborate articles (July 15, 1974; November 8, 1976; August 6, 1979). To be sure, forceful leadership, or its absence, is a key factor in explaining the success or failure of any enterprise, including the Church and her universities. As *Time* stated in 1979, "Leadership involves combinations of the inspirational and the managerial."[8] It does, indeed, and when these are missing there is serious danger of drift in the day-to-day operation of any institution.

In the case of the Catholic University of America, the generation that followed James H. Ryan's departure in 1935 might be said to bear some resemblance to an era of *recteurs fainéants* after the fashion of the Frankish kings of the seventh century. I do not mean to suggest that these men were lazy and accomplished nothing for the institution; yet the combination of inspirational and managerial talents alluded to by *Time* were not in evidence. Patrick McCormick was conscientous and dutiful in the exercise of his office, but his highly conservative nature forbade him to venture onto untried paths, although as I have said, he did

---

[7]John Henry Newman, *The Idea of A University*. London: Longmans, Green and Company. 1923. p. 471.

[8]"A Cry for Leadership," *Time*, 114 (August 6, 1979), 27.

not stand in the way of others doing so. We all have our limitations, and there are vast areas of human activity where any man or woman may fail simply because they do not possess the qualities that make for genuine leadership. Thus the old adage, *nemo dat quod non habet*, applies to each of us in one context or another and should not be applied only to university rectors and presidents. The blame in cases of this kind frequently rests as much, and probably more, on those whose votes bring the poorly qualified to such important posts.

Bishop McCormick was a man who had enjoyed excellent health through most of his life, a condition that he may have attributed in part to his regular practice of golfing. In the spring of 1953, however, he took ill, and in about six weeks he died of cancer on May 18 at the age of seventy-three. After an interim of less than six weeks—an uncommonly quick transition—he was succeeded by Bryan J. McEntegart, who for the previous ten years had been Bishop of Ogdensburg, New York. After his education for the priesthood this tall and rather portly man had pursued graduate studies in sociology and social work at the Catholic University of America and the New York School of Social Work. His tenure of the rectorship was relatively brief, less than four years, since in April, 1957, he was named Bishop of Brooklyn.

My early relations with Bishop McEntegart were quite cordial. He seemed genuinely pleased when I was invited to give the Walgreen Lectures at the University of Chicago in January, 1955, and remarked, "Good, and you are not a Jesuit," or words to that effect. Precisely what he meant I did not know and did not ask. I have often said that for me more light is thrown on persons and events by little episodes than by lengthy discourses. In that regard I found a chance remark of Bishop McEntegart's more revealing perhaps of his mind than his addresses and sermons delivered at formal academic occasions. The Archbishop of Cape Town, South

Africa, Owen McCann, was a guest for dinner one evening in Curley Hall. As I rose to leave the dining room the rector called to me and said he wished to introduce me to the visitor. After a brief exchange of pleasantries we reached the door of the chapel, whereupon the rector leaned over to the archbishop and whispered, "This fellow writes books."

I do not wish to read too much into the remark, but I could not help think that this would hardly be the way in which Nathan Pusey, President of Harvard in those days, might have introduced a visitor in Cambridge to, let us say, Samuel Eliot Morison. It told me more than I cared to know. It is possible that a remark of this kind was meant as humor and that I should not have taken it seriously. Yet I found it difficult to dissociate it from an attitude that was scarcely calculated to lend encouragement to the scholarly endeavor that university professors were generally expected to pursue.

What had begun as a friendly relationship between Bishop McEntegart and me gradually cooled, and before his death in 1968 I learned from a reliable source that he did not wish to have my name mentioned in his presence. The chain of events that brought about this attitude opened with an invitation I received in 1954 to read a paper at the tenth International Congress of Historical Sciences in Rome scheduled for September, 1955. The invitation from Professor Myron P. Gilmore of Harvard, chairman of the American committee for the congress, specified that they wished me to speak to the Catholic Church and Church-State relations in the United States. At the time there was sharp controversy in American Catholic circles on that subject with John Courtney Murray, S.J., of Woodstock College making a strong defense of the American system of separation of Church and State, and Joseph C. Fenton and Francis J. Connell, C.SS.R., theologians at the Catholic University of America, just as stoutly contending that the American practice was not reconcilable with the teaching of the Holy See, a position which they elaborated in the pages of the *American Ecclesiastical Review*, of which Fenton was then editor.

When the Gilmore letter arrived I asked permission of my ordinary, Archbishop Patrick A. O'Boyle, to accept the invitation. Parenthetically, today such permission would probably not be sought, but ecclesiastical discipline was much tighter a generation ago. The archbishop, of course, was painfully aware of the Murray-Fenton feud and quite understandably he delayed a decision until he could discuss the matter with the rector who was then on his way home from Europe. Soon after McEntegart's return I received a call from the archbishop asking me to come for lunch. I suspected the result, namely, his request that I forego the reading of the paper at the Rome congress.

I accepted the decision and that was the last heard about it until 1963 when the then rector, Monsignor William J. McDonald, McEntegart's successor, took the unusual step of banning four distinguished theologians from speaking at the university since, it was said, they represented only one side of certain controversial questions then under discussion at Vatican Council II. The men in question were: Godfrey Diekmann, O.S.B., Hans Küng, John Courtney Murray, S. J., and Gustav Weigel, S.J.[9] When the news broke it became an immediate *cause célèbre* in Catholic circles with the non-Catholic press likewise carrying news stories across the land. In the midst of the tension created by the banning I received a call from Father John M. Joyce, then editor of the Catholic weekly of the Diocese of Oklahoma City and Tulsa, who inquired what I thought about the matter. I deplored the action of the rector, and I added that this sort of thing had been going on at the university for over a decade. To employ what one of my church historian friends says is one of my favorite expressions, I would be less than

[9]For further details of this case, see Donald E. Pelotte, S.S.S., *John Courtney Murray. Theologian in Conflict*. New York: Paulist Press. 1975.

honest if I were to pretend that the McEntegart refusal for the Rome paper in 1954 was not then in my mind. My statement, of course, carried the story back to the McEntegart administration, and the Bishop of Brooklyn was furious. He wrote me a strong letter of protest, and finding my reply unsatisfactory, he asked the Board of Trustees at their meeting in November, 1963, to adopt a resolution of censure of me. The effort failed, but thereafter it came as no surprise to hear every once in a while rumbles of the bishop's ire in my regard.

3

California and Texas

While on the subject of the bishops who headed the university between 1927 and 1957, I should like to mention several other prelates whom I came to know as a member of the faculty of the university's branch summer sessions in San Rafael, California, and San Antonio, Texas. I taught at Dominican College, San Rafael, in the summers of 1933 and 1934 at a time when Edward J. Hanna, Archbishop of San Francisco, was in his declining years. This first chairman of the National Catholic Welfare Conference was a gracious and irenic personality who had ruled the See of San Francisco since 1915. I came to know him on his periodic visits to San Rafael when he would take dinner with us in the faculty dining room. He was unfailingly pleasant, agreeable, and entirely approachable, a widely beloved figure in the Bay Area, and that by men and women of any and of no religious persuasion. In a word, Archbishop Hanna was a conspicuous figure in civic as well as ecclesiastical affairs who had endeared himself to a large and varied circle of friends and admirers.

By the time I came to know him, however, he was seventy-four and time had taken its inevitable toll. That fact became evident one evening in July, 1934, when the archbishop dined with us in the midst of the grave general strike that had virtually paralyzed San Francisco the previous weekend, a strike that was initiated by the Pacific Coast District of the International Longshoremen's Association headed by the formidable Harry Bridges, the Australian-born labor leader. In the crisis President Roosevelt appointed a board of mediation and named Hanna as its chairman. The strike attracted national attention and little else was on San Francisco's mind during those tense days. We were naturally curious to get the archbishop's reaction, and during dinner we asked him how the mediation efforts were going. I recall his answer almost verbatim. "Well," he said, "Mr. Bridges is so serious. I say to him, 'smile for the archbishop,' and that helps to relieve the tension." Knowing Bridges' reputation for toughness, we could only glance at one another in wonderment that an invitation to smile might be of much use in those grim proceedings. It was evident that Archbishop Hanna had passed his peak and that the elderly churchman who had smoothed over many a dispute in former times was scarcely equal to his present assignment. Less than a year later Hanna resigned and retired to Rome where he lived on until 1944 amid the disability caused by a steadily increasing senility.

It was only a generation after I first met Archbishop Hanna that I came to learn a good deal about him from his former secretary, Monsignor Thomas F. Millett, during the year (1963-1964) that I lived at Saint Agnes Rectory. While Millett was fundamentally loyal to Hanna's memory, he made it clear that the prelate's amiability often caused real problems such as promises made but left unfulfilled and difficult situations allowed to drag on without a remedy. Be that as it may, Edward Hanna was a lovable man whose personal charm I experienced at first hand. My last meeting with him came one evening in that summer of 1934 when he entertained us at dinner with tales of his experiences of one kind or another. At the end of the meal Mother Raymond O'Connor, general superior of the Dominican sisters, came to greet him, and the final picture of the archbishop that remains with me is that of the old churchman strolling down the long corridor of the administration building arm in arm with Mother Raymond, his good friend, as they went off for a private chat.

If those responsible for the appointment of Hanna's successor had sought to find one who offered a strong contrast, they could not have improved on their choice of John J. Mitty, like Hanna, a New Yorker, who had served for six years as Bishop of Salt Lake City. Mitty had been a chaplain in World War I and his approach resembled that of a military commander. He was efficient, hard working, thoroughly dedicated, and what one might accurately describe as 'tough.' Today he would answer to the current expression of a 'no-nonsense' man. I met him several times in San Rafael when he was coadjutor to Hanna and, too, on later

Californians: Mayor Rossi of San Francisco, Archbishop Hanna, Governor Rolph and Archbishop Mitty.

occasions when I would visit San Francisco. I never felt any
warmth at these meetings, and I got the idea that he would
be happier if I would withdraw and allow him to return to
his work desk. The same was true of our infrequent meetings
at the university. At his death in 1961 Archbishop Mitty left
a huge sum of money in the archdiocese's possession, due in
good measure to his financial skill and to his close husband-
ing of financial resources. In fact, his reputation in that
regard was so marked that he earned the nickname, 'work
without pay.' Yet if he was stern in manner he was also
far-sighted in such things as the education of his priests. I
frequently noted the large number of priests of the Archdiocese of San Francisco who were sent to the university for
graduate studies in his time. As a consequence when he died
San Francisco was about as well supplied with a properly
trained clergy as any American diocese.

John Mitty was not, however, a man noted for breadth of
mind in all intellectual matters. For example, some time
after the publication of my life of Cardinal Gibbons in 1952
I was told of his chagrin at the openness with which I had
related disputes among the bishops of Gibbons' generation.
I found these rumors disturbing, especially when I was told
that Mitty had stated that he would see to it that no historian would do that to him, for he intended to destroy his
papers. The rumor was confirmed when I related what I had
heard to Robert J. Dwyer, then Bishop of Reno, only to
have the latter declare, "Yes, it is true, he told me so himself." After moving to San Francisco in 1963 I pursued the
subject with the archdiocesan chancellor, Donnell A.
Walsh, and I was vastly relieved when he told me that he had
asked the late archbishop's secretary, Miss Helen Quinan,
who stated that Mitty had indeed intended to destroy all his
papers, "but he never got around to doing so."

After the two summers in California I was asked to
assume direction of the university's newly established southern branch summer session in San Antonio. There the two

Catholic women's colleges—Our Lady of the Lake and
Incarnate Word—were in such keen rivalry that the university did not dare to choose one or the other but yielded to the
rather ridiculous compromise of locating the session in
both. As a consequence I had to make daily trips across
town in order to keep office hours at both campuses. It was
not a very pleasant task considering the intense heat of
Texas in July and August. I lived in the rectory at Our Lady
of the Lake College and took my meals with the Oblate
Fathers who served as chaplains. At the time the Archbishop of San Antonio was Arthur J. Drossaerts, a Dutch-
born churchman who had come to San Antonio in 1918
after nearly thirty years of parochial ministry in the Archdiocese of New Orleans. Drossaerts, then in his early seven-
ties, was a gentle soul who gave evidence of a certain
euphoria not uncommon to men of his age. He steered clear
as much as possible of the inevitable controversies and
disputes that arose from time to time within his flock.

Archbishop Drossaerts came to the college fairly frequently, and after dinner we would sit on the rectory's
screened porch and visit in the long summer evenings. One
night I brashly asked him if he did not think it would be a
good thing for Catholic higher education in San Antonio if
the two colleges were to merge, or at least work out a
program of close co-operation. He smiled benignly and
replied, "You are a very young man, Doctor. I would not
touch them with a ten-foot pole." It was obvious that no
solution to the awkward situation was to be expected from
the local ordinary. Drossaerts was a very friendly man, and
one who in today's parlance would probably be called 'a
father figure.' I enjoyed sounding out the old gentleman on
his varied experiences. At that time the persecution of the
Church in Mexico by the Calles and Portes Gil regimes was
still at its height, and among the large number of exiles then
living in San Antonio was the Archbishop of Morelia and
Apostolic Delegate, Leopoldo Ruíz y Flores. I was a guest

at dinner on one occasion at Incarnate Word College with
Archbishop Drossaerts and the Mexican prelate who, I
recall, gave me an inscribed picture of Our Lady of Guada-
lupe which I kept for many years. Since I had only a superficial knowledge of the Mexican situation, I was glad to learn
more that night from listening to Ruíz y Flores and Drossaerts exchange views.

Michael J. Curley

It is understandable that those bishops I came to know really well should have lived in Washington or in the general region of the national capital. It was there that I knew six of the nine bishops who served as rectors of the university, and it was there that I knew the university's second chancellor, Michael J. Curley, Archbishop of Baltimore, and his three successors in that office. I saw the chancellor at various functions during my first years at the university, and it was he who presided at the commencement in June, 1928, when I received my M.A. degree. This Irish-born prelate had been named Bishop of Saint Augustine, Florida, in 1914 at the age of thirty-four, and seven years later he was promoted to the premier See of Baltimore following the death of Cardinal Gibbons. At that time the chancellor of the university was *ex officio* the Archbishop of Baltimore, as since 1948 he has been the Archbishop of Washington.

It has been said that readers have a right to expect in autobiography what they get in a good novel, and especially that which pertains to characterization. The point is a valid one, even if it is difficult to achieve with true accuracy. It is easy enough to describe Michael Curley's commanding presence—tall, handsome, eloquent, forceful in both appearance and in speech. Once he began to address an audience one listened regardless of whether or not one agreed with what he was saying. He was fearless to a degree that at times gave the impression of brashness, and occasionally even with a suggestion of arrogance. Yet the external bravura cloaked, I believe, an inner shyness and feeling of inferiority, particularly when dealing with those he thought his superiors in intelligence and knowledge. For example, the day he introduced Joseph Corrigan to the faculty of the Catholic University of America as the new rector in the spring of 1936, he stated he would read the papal brief of appointment, and he added, "It is in Latin; for those of you who do not understand Latin, let someone translate it for you."

Michael Curley was a man of quick temper and deep-seated likes and dislikes. He felt a special distaste for President Franklin Roosevelt and his policies, and on frequent occasions he did not hesitate to say so publicly. In one instance this sentiment carried the archbishop beyond his own better judgment. It was Sunday, December 7, 1941, and he had been confirming in western Maryland and returned to Baltimore without having learned of the attack on Pearl Harbor. Soon after reaching his Charles Street residence a reporter appeared and asked what he thought of the war in the Pacific. "War in the Pacific?" he queried, "We have a war in the Atlantic and we might as well have one in the Pacific!" When he became aware of the true situation he made an apology, one of the few times that Curley publicly acknowledged having been in error.

I came to know the Archbishop of Baltimore very well during the last years of his life. The circumstances were these. It was in the spring of 1945 that I decided to write the life of his distinguished predecessor, James Gibbons, and, of course, I had to seek permission to use the vast Gibbons Papers in the archdiocesan archives. Through the kindly intervention of Monsignor Joseph M. Nelligan, chancellor of the archdiocese, the archbishop was approached and readily gave his consent. I shall always remember my meeting with the latter in regard to the Gibbons biography. He said he understood that I wanted to write the life of the cardinal and he stated he was altogether willing that I should have full access to the sources. He then added, "I did not approve of Cardinal Gibbons. When I came here to Baltimore I found the atmosphere saturated with liberalism." It was a rather grave charge that I was then in no position to refute, even though I seriously doubted it from the outset. I later repeated the remark to the Baltimore-born Peter L. Ireton, Bishop of Richmond, who immediately retorted, "Its a damn lie!" If it was not a 'lie' it was at least a mistaken judgment of which I became fully convinced as I continued my research. Yet to Curley's credit it should be said that he gave me complete freedom and never once interfered or even questioned me about any phase of the work. In that respect I enjoyed the same kind of freedom as Monsignor John A. Ryan, professor of moral theology in the Catholic University of America, with whose ideas Curley thoroughly disagreed; yet he let it be known that as long as he was chancellor of the university Ryan was at liberty to write and to speak as he thought fit. A scholar cannot ask for more than this from his academic superiors, even if he or she might be gratified by a warmer approval of their work.

By the time I began my research on the Gibbons biography in early July, 1945, Archbishop Curley's health was already in decline. I was compelled to spend weeks at a time at 408 North Charles Street, the archiepiscopal residence, where the archives were then housed. We met at table daily and during the course of those many months we became, I think I can honestly say, good friends. He loved to banter, to utter provocative statements and to test reactions from those around the table. I soon caught on to this tactic and, in turn, enjoyed putting loaded questions to him that enabled

Apostolic Delegate Cicognani with Archbishop Curley, March 25, 1940 at the occasion of the latter's installation as Archbishop of Washington.

him to expostulate at length about controversial matters, and *en passant*, to give off piquant remarks about some of his fellow bishops. I recall one day I sought to draw him out about the relations between Cardinals O'Connell and Mundelein; but this time His Grace felt the ice was getting too thin, for he suddenly rose from the table and exclaimed, "We'll be going now!" At first I had felt a sense of awe in the presence of this commanding figure, but as time wore on I overcame my shyness and thoroughly enjoyed our frequent exchanges. In the last months of his life Archbishop Curley was virtually blind, and now and then I would go in the evenings to chat with him in his room before returning to Washington. One night after a brief visit I stated I would have to be going home. "Very well," he said, "come back whenever you like, and when we get tired of you, we'll throw you out!" I knew by that time how to interpret this rough language.

One evening in mid-May of 1947 I was working alone in the archives when the telephone rang. The voice identified itself as that of Sister Helena of Bon Secours Hospital, and she asked for Monsignor Nelligan. I told her that he and all the priests were out, whereupon she left a message for Nelligan to call the hospital. I knew Sister Helena was the archbishop's nurse and wondered to myself if the call pertained to him. In a few minutes another call came and Joe Nelligan told me that the archbishop had had a stroke. Knowing that the chancellor would be out late I put a note on his pillow that I would offer the 6:30 Mass the following morning so that he could sleep later. The next morning I rose and went to the cathedral only to find Monsignor Nelligan vesting for Mass. I asked how the archbishop was and was startled to have him reply, "He is dead." At that I remarked I would go out to his altar and offer Mass for the repose of his soul.

I had more on my mind at the moment, I confess, than the death of Michael Curley. Some weeks before I had decided to seek incardination into the Archdiocese of Baltimore and Washington—they were then united under Curley. The latter agreed without hesitation, and it happened that I took the oath in the chancery about 5 o'clock on the afternoon of May 16 from Joe Nelligan who stated he would take the papers to the hospital to be signed by the archbishop and that would complete my transfer from the Diocese of Winona to the Archdiocese of Washington. Parenthetically, the papers were made out for Washington alone, not for Baltimore and Washington, which was a signal of their approaching separation. In any case, as I started toward the cabinet to vest for Mass on the morning of May 17 Joe called across the sacristy to me, "The last thing he did was to sign your papers." He had signed my incardination papers about 7:30 in the evening, the stroke came around 9, and by 11 o'clock he was dead. At the funeral one of the priests whispered to me, "I hear you killed our archbishop."

I have dwelt at some length on my relationship to Archbishop Curley since I had come to have a real affection for this gruff churchman whose genuine virtues were hidden to many. One of those virtues was generosity. I think especially of his turning over his silver jubilee gift of over $200,000 to the Sulpicians for Saint Mary's Seminary, a society of priests whom he admired but to whom, as he said, he owed nothing. The American Sulpicians have more than once acknowledged that Michael Curley was their most generous benefactor, and this was only a single example of his generosity. In a word, Archbishop Curley was a true churchman—dutiful, hard working, an example of simplicity in his lifestyle, even though he was likewise on occasion brash in speech, blunt, and seemingly harsh on some with whom he disagreed.

While no one who knew Michael Curley would question his basic goodness and his fidelity to the Church, his appointment to Baltimore in August, 1921, was not well received, and that by more than William T. Russell, the Baltimore-born Bishop of Charleston, who had hoped to be named as Gibbons' successor. How had the appointment come about? No one lacking access to the pertinent Roman archives for that time can answer the question with finality. Yet the fact that the Apostolic Delegate to the United States had then, and has now, a commanding voice in the selection of American bishops, sheds some light on the matter. The delegate in 1921 was Archbishop Giovanni Bonzano who was professor and rector of the Urban College of Propaganda during the years that Curley was a student in Rome. I further heard it said that on a visit to Florida, Bonzano heard Curley preach and was much impressed, and that the latter's ability in the pulpit was common knowledge there was no doubt.

In any case, Curley's promotion was something less than ideal as a successor to Cardinal Gibbons who had left such a strong imprint not only on Baltimore but on the nation at large. As I have said, Curley did not approve of the cardinal, and not long after his arrival in the Maryland metropolis he declared from the cathedral pulpit, "I have not come to Baltimore to be archbishop to Baltimore's first families." The Shriver family, to whom Gibbons had been especially close, felt this keenly, as two of their number informed me during an interview on their relationship to Cardinal Gibbons. The fact that Curley was Irish-born was not helpful, for of all the dioceses in the United States the premier see might well have been thought the proper place for a native-born son. As I had reason to know, Archbishop Curley suffered the 'slings and arrows' of ill fortune that befall most of humankind, and one time when we were discussing the career of a certain disappointed churchman, he suddenly exclaimed, "Rome will use you, abuse you, and then throw you away!" I could not help but think that there was an autobiographical strain in the remark. More than Michael Curley have been tempted to say as much.

5

Minnesota Ordinaries

Having spoken of my transfer to the Archdiocese of Washington in May, 1947, I wish to say something about the two bishops who were my ordinaries between 1938 and 1947. The circumstances were as follows. In September, 1932, I began teaching history at the College of Saint Teresa in Winona, Minnesota, and it was during this time that I decided to study for the priesthood. I was then twenty-eight years of age, a layman with a Ph.D. in church history, who had no previous training for the priesthood beyond several college courses in religion and philosophy. I did not know the bishop of my native diocese, Peoria, and I was informed that Cardinal Mundelein, in whose archdiocese I had worked for several summers, would not incardinate me for Chicago since I had not studied at Quigley Preparatory Seminary.

Where, then, was I to find a bishop? I consulted with my best priest friend in Winona, Joseph F. Hale, then chancellor and chaplain at Saint Teresa's. I asked him if he thought the Bishop of Winona, Francis M. Kelly, would adopt me, and he answered that I might try. In any case, I made an appointment with the bishop for a Sunday afternoon in the

53

spring of 1934 and went out to his residence on the hill neighboring Saint Mary's College. The tall, handsome, and soft-spoken prelate received me kindly and listened without interruption to my story. I told him that I wished to teach rather than to do parish work, to which he raised no objection. At that point he inquired how the seminary expenses were to be met, and I assured him that I would pay my own way by teaching in the summers. He then stated, "If I understand you correctly, Mr. Ellis, you wish to use the Diocese of Winona as a means to your end." This, I thought, is the time for plain speaking and I said, yes, that was what I had in mind, expecting that he would say that he could not agree to my proposal. I was no little surprised when he quietly remarked, "I see no difficulty in that arrangement."

Bishop Kelly then asked if I would like to study at the North American College in Rome, of which both he and Joe Hale were graduates. I assured him that I recognized the advantages that Rome would offer, but by reason of the straitened finances of my family my only brother, Norbert, would have to drop out of college if I did not remain in the United States to assist my father in paying his expenses. The bishop accepted my explanation with his customary serenity, but Joe Hale was distinctly annoyed at my having declined the chance to study in Rome. "You can borrow the money, can't you?" he exclaimed. I suppose I could have done so but I was not disposed to go into debt if it could be avoided. If my friend remained for sometime unreconciled to my decision he ultimately forgave what he considered my lack of vision and agreed to tutor me privately that spring in those courses in philosophy that I had missed in college.

I left Winona in June, 1934, and in September entered the Sulpician Seminary in Washington. From time to time I returned to Minnesota, and it was there that Bishop Kelly ordained me with two others to the priesthood in the Chapel of Our Lady of the Angels at the College of Saint Teresa on June 5, 1938. I found the bishop unfailingly kind and when

he came to Washington to the annual meeting of the hierarchy he would take me out to dinner and I, in turn, would
visit him when in Winona. He was criticized by some of his
priests—what bishop has ever escaped?—for his do-nothing
policies, so to speak, but I never had any reason to complain
about him. His lack of energy may have been due in part to
his health, for about 1940 he began to decline and in the
following years he suffered repeated strokes that left him
completely incapacitated, and I recall that the last time I saw
Bishop Kelly in Saint Mary's Hospital in Rochester, Minnesota, he could neither speak nor walk, and I even wondered
if he knew who I was. This condition occasioned the
appointment of a coadjutor *c.j.s.*, in 1942 in the person of
Monsignor Leo Binz, one of the secretaries at the Apostolic
Delegation. Meanwhile Francis Kelly lingered on until
death ended his long ordeal in June, 1950.

My relationship to Bishop Binz was equally cordial. I
recall my visit to him in December, 1942, while he was on
retreat at the Sulpician Seminary for his ordination to the
episcopacy, and my attendance at his ordination in Rockford, Illinois, his home diocese, later that month. During
our visit at the seminary he was not only friendly but sur-
prisingly open. I remember his asking me if I thought Father
Hale would like to do graduate work, and I answered that I
thought he would. In the event Joe Hale was sent by Binz to
the Catholic University of America where he took his
J.C.D. degree and then returned to Winona where he was
once again chancellor and ultimately vicar general and Rector of Sacred Heart Cathedral. In fact, unless my memory is
playing tricks on me, that same evening Binz remarked that
Hale would make a good bishop. I heartily agreed and in the
following years his name was frequently mentioned for the
episcopacy. The years passed, however, and nothing happened. There can be no doubt that his normally cheerful
disposition changed in his last years, but whether or not
disappointment was the cause, I frankly do not know. When

he died suddenly on October 1, 1957, on the eve of his fifty-first birthday there were those who felt that disillusionment had hastened his end. Joe Hale was an exemplary priest, and if the speculations were true it did not seriously detract from his fine priestly attainments. He was surely not the first priest—nor the last—who may have believed that his talents had not been recognized and rewarded. He was the deacon at my first solemn Mass in Saint Patrick's Church in Seneca on June 12, 1938, and to the end I entertained a genuine esteem and fondness for this good friend.

I have strayed from Bishop Binz in recounting my association with Joe Hale. During the five years that Leo Binz was my ordinary he was always kindness itself. As in the case of Bishop Kelly, we exchanged visits in Washington and Winona when the opportunity presented itself. When I determined on changing dioceses he expressed his regret at my departure but readily gave his assent to the transfer. Unacquainted as I was with the procedure of canon law, I was surprised at the number of official documents that the transaction entailed, and I always retained a sense of gratitude for the consideration shown me by the Coadjutor Bishop of Winona in sending all the papers addressed to Archbishop Curley first to me in stamped and unsealed envelopes for me to read before forwarding them to Baltimore. It was a small matter, to be sure, but as has so often been said, life is made up of small things, and I appreciated the courtesy. After the completion of the transfer one of the Winona priests remarked that although Binz was sorry to see me go, there was a measure of joy in it for him since it gave him—a canon lawyer—his first chance to use the canon on the excardination of a priest!

Leo Binz left Winona in 1949 when promoted to Dubuque, then in December, 1961, he was again promoted in being named Archbishop of Saint Paul where he remained until his resignation in 1975. He died in October, 1979, at the age of seventy-nine. We met occasionally between 1947 and his retirement, especially during the years he served as a trustee of the university when he would remain overnight in Curley Hall and we would take breakfast together. As in the case of all bishops, Binz had his critics, but once again my personal relationship was never other than friendly with this prelate who, like myself, was a native of northern Illinois. In saying this I do not wish to give an exaggerated impression of cordiality, for I lived most of the time at a distance of nearly 1,000 miles from Kelly and Binz. Had I been at close range it might have been quite different, as it was from time to time with those bishops with whom I was in closer communication.

6

Baltimore-Born

Among this group I was probably on more intimate terms with John M. McNamara, first Auxiliary Bishop of Baltimore and later Auxiliary Bishop of Washington, than any other in those years. His appointment to the episcopacy in 1928 came a decade or two before a notable development in the American hierarchy in the spiraling number of auxiliary bishops. Their numbers reflect, of course, the growth among lay Catholics and the necessity to provide for the latter's spiritual needs. The first American auxiliary bishop as such—earlier there had been several coadjutor bishops with the right of succession—was the convert Sylvester Rosecrans who was appointed in 1861 as auxiliary to Archbishop John B. Purcell of Cincinnati. He was a brother of William Rosecrans, the Civil War general who had entered the Church while teaching at West Point. In any case, of the 380 bishops of the United States at the present writing (July 1, 1983), 105 are auxiliaries.[10] If they are now too numerous

---

[10]As of July 1, 1983, there were 176 archdioceses and dioceses in the United States with 169 ordinaries; six sees were then vacant; 105 auxiliary bishops, 2 coadjutors, and 89 retired bishops.

for all ultimately to become ordinaries of the nation's 176 dioceses, a considerable percentage still have, and will probably continue to have, that prospect.

The system has both advantages and disadvantages. For example, Rosecrans was chosen in 1868 as the first Bishop of Columbus and served the diocese well for ten years. But if a man of mediocre talents is selected he can become more of a burden than a blessing to his original diocese, and *a fortiori* to the diocese of which he is named ordinary. In the past much has depended, and presumably still depends, on the initiative and motivation of the ordinary who submits a priest's name for auxiliary bishop. Yet this has not always been true, for certainly Cardinal William O'Connell of Boston had not chosen, nor did he approve, of the auxiliary bishop sent to him in September, 1932, in the person of Francis J. Spellman.

Normally, however, the choice arises with the ordinary, and here the Church's history reveals many instances where outstanding prelates could not, nonetheless, bring themselves to advance a priest of superior quality lest the latter should outshine them. In that connection one thinks of Henry Edward Manning, Cardinal Archbishop of Westminster, who in 1879 sought to prevent Newman from being named a cardinal. Manning was unquestionably an outstanding churchman, but in his reckoning England was not large enough for two red hats. Nor has American Catholic history been without its share of cases of this kind, for example, when in 1900 perhaps the most learned bishop the American hierarchy has ever known, John Lancaster Spalding of Peoria, chose as auxiliary the Irish-born Peter J. O'Reilly who lent little if any lustre to the episcopacy during Spalding's declining years.

Not long ago a high ranking prelate remarked to me that he thought there were too many auxiliary bishops in the United States. He exclaimed, "They are lined up like cars in a parking lot!" Their number is probably higher here in relation to the Catholic population than in most countries. But with American Catholics now in excess of 51,000,000 it is obvious, for example, that ordinaries of the 7 archdioceses and 2 dioceses each with over a million Catholics, not to mention a dozen more with between 500,000 and 1,000,000 members each would have need of them, especially if the practice is maintained of having only bishops confer the sacrament of confirmation. Be that as it may, the tradition would seem to have established itself pretty firmly in the American Church and I doubt it will be reversed without a struggle.

This digression on auxiliary bishops has been prompted by those of that rank who were well known to me, among whom, I have said, John McNamara was *facile princeps*. If the appointment of this Baltimore-born churchman illustrated the principle of 'not outshining the ordinary,' it was, nevertheless, an altogether admirable choice. He was forty-nine years of age at the time and had for some years been pastor of Saint Gabriel's Church in Washington where he continued to reside until his death in 1960. Although I was a graduate student in Washington at the time of his appointment, I cannot recall having met him until about 1940, but that first meeting was an unforgettable one. I had preached the sermon on the patronal feast of Saint Patrick's Church in downtown Washington, and after the Mass my friend, John Cartwright, came to me and said I should meet the bishop. Following the introduction I was slightly startled to have McNamara exclaim, "Why do you university professors, you and Ignatius Smith, shout so? You do not have to shout to be heard in this church." I cannot remember what I replied, if I replied at all, but it was something less than an auspicious beginning for what in time turned out to be an enduring and affectionate relationship. If I had heard that John McNamara was given to candid speech, I now had first hand evidence of the fact.

In that connection years later I learned of how McNamara employed this candor with his ordinary, Cardinal Gibbons. The latter always stopped at Saint Patrick's when in Washington, and one morning the then Father McNamara, who had for some years been assigned to a rural parish in southern Maryland, was asked to serve the cardinal's Mass. In the middle of the Mass the pastor called McNamara out to send him on some errand. At breakfast Gibbons said, "You do not know your ceremonies, Sir. You left me in the middle of Mass and did not return." Whereupon McNamara replied, "If Your Eminence had not left me so long in the country I might know my ceremonies better." I was astonished at the blunt reply to the venerable cardinal and asked McNamara how the former had taken it, only to be told that he simply smiled and went on with his breakfast. If it said much about Mack's candor, it said as much if not more about Gibbons' benignity in dealing with his young priests.

Bishop Mack, as we frequently referred to him, was a first rate preacher in his own right, one who, it was said, spoke 'with a tear in his voice,' a feature that made him all the more appealing. Moreover, he had a special gift for talking to children, so much so that adults used to frequent the 9 o'clock Sunday Mass at Saint Gabriel's to listen to him preach to the youngsters. I once asked him how he had gone about perfecting his preaching skills. Every preacher of the Word of God might profitably ponder his simple answer. He said, "When I was a young priest stationed at Saint Patrick's Church here in Washington I was often assigned the 9 o'clock Sunday Mass. I would ascend the pulpit and look down into the two big blue eyes of Senator Thomas J. Walsh of Montana, and I would say to myself, 'now you can't fool him.'" It was a wise observation that I never forgot and, I hope, tried to emulate. He never failed to leave a marked impression on his audiences, and I recall how immensely proud I was at the luncheon on January 13, 1948, that followed the episcopal ordination in Saint Patrick's Cathedral, New York, of Patrick A. O'Boyle, a ceremony to which I had accompanied Bishop McNamara. There were about a half dozen speakers that day, but Mack outshone them all in a happy blend of history and spiritual exhortation that left a lasting memory, and that was but a single instance, for there were many others.

John McNamara was a deeply spiritual man of exemplary priestly bearing, as well as one who constantly improved his mind by serious reading. He would be the first to say that he was not a scholar, but he appreciated cultivation of mind in others. In fact, at times he was more respectful of real or presumed learning than may have been deserved. John Cartwright, Louis Arand, and I were often guests for dinner at Saint Gabriel's, and on one occasion he told his three assistant priests that we were coming for dinner and they should remain silent and learn from the conversation of the guests! It was a preconciliar approach that would today probably meet with stout remonstrance.

As time passed I felt much freer in my relations with the bishop, and that to a point where I sometimes overstepped what he thought were the bounds of propriety. More than once my brashness gave offense, and I always remember being told by the late John B. Roeder, one of the bishop's assistants, that on the occasion of the episcopal ordination of John J. Russell as Bishop of Charleston in March, 1950, McNamara remarked to Roeder, "I met Ellis at the Mayflower but I was cool toward him; he is too fresh," or words to that effect. I was always ultimately forgiven, however, and we would resume our customary friendly association.

During the repeated illnesses of Archbishop Curley, John McNamara as vicar general would frequently spend some days at the archbishop's house in Baltimore, and while I was working there on the life of Cardinal Gibbons we had many walks and intimate chats in which this normally discreet churchman would now and then open up, as he did the day he told me he would have liked to have been named Archbishop of Washington (but not of Baltimore), although he realized that his age—he was then seventy—was against him. Speaking of those days together at 408 North Charles Street in Baltimore, reminds me of one of the most embarrassing *faux pas* of my entire life. During the evening meal I was seated at the bishop's right and Father Joseph Manns, one of the cathedral assistants, came in, sat opposite me at table, and stated, "There has been a man of your name appointed a bishop" (it was Edward Ellis as Bishop of Nottingham in England). To that piece of news I made inquiry, "Is he a bishop or only an auxiliary?" There was a painful silence during which I wished that the floor might open and take me out of sight, but the bishop said nothing and after the awkward pause the conversation was resumed on some other topic. I have had more than my share of such blunders, but that was about the worst I can recall.

Like most of us, Bishop McNamara had his favorites, as well as those whom he did not fancy, and one of the latter for reasons unknown to me was the university rector, Patrick McCormick. One evening when visiting with the bishop at Saint Gabriel's I stated that news had come that day that McCormick had been appointed to a second term, whereupon Mack while going out the door quietly remarked, "And he voted for himself." By reason of the numerous religious houses of study in Washington, most of which at the time were crowded with candidates, he was the ordaining prelate for an enormous number of deacons and priests—I received all my own orders up to priesthood at his hands in the crypt church of the National Shrine of the Immaculate Conception—and he was proud of the fact that he was getting fairly close to the record of Cardinal Gibbons in that regard. Gibbons had ordained 2,471 priests, a number that has yet to be exceeded in the American Church.

I had a deep affection for Bishop McNamara and I was truly grieved when he died in November, 1960, after an illness of only two days. I recall weeping at the funeral in Saint Matthew's Cathedral at the moving eulogy preached by Monsignor Cartwright. I made the trip to the provincial house of the Daughters of Charity of Saint Vincent de Paul in Emmitsburg, Maryland, where he had asked to be buried alongside the remains of Elizabeth Seton in the little mausoleum in the community cemetery. It was a fitting resting place for John McNamara, to be sure, for no one had done more to further the beatification of Mother Seton than he had. He traveled repeatedly to the widespread mother-houses of the communities that traced their roots to Elizabeth Seton, and by his persistent exhortation and persuasive eloquence ultimately achieved a unity among these religious women who had hitherto gone their separate ways with little or no co-operation among them. In fact, it was remarked that the bishop's success in rallying them to joint action all the way from Emmitsburg to Halifax, Nova Scotia, with Missouri, Ohio, New Jersey, and New York in between, was the first miracle earned in Seton's name! Although he had already gone to God, John McNamara's name was in frequent mention by those who knew the background when Seton was beatified in 1963 and again on September 14, 1975, at the canonization of the first native American saint.

Two other Baltimore-born bishops who were well known to me were John S. Spence and Peter L. Ireton. But aside from their birthplace and their episcopal rank, they had little in common, for their temperaments and life style were vastly different. I came to really know Spence during the years that I helped out on weekends at Saint Matthew's Cathedral where he was then in residence. He was intelligent, hard working, and dedicated, to be sure; but for many his good qualities were in part nullified by his pomposity. In a word, John Spence took himself very seriously, an inhibiting characteristic in any one no matter what his or her rank may be. Yet it would be unfair to leave a wholly negative impression of the man. True, his manner would in the 1980's invite from many either stark incredulity or open derision. But those who knew him best, while aware of the man's weaknesses, were likewise aware of his virtues—generosity, consideration for others, and devotedness to any task entrusted to him.

This last characteristic became evident to me in the spring of 1950 when he was put in charge of the Holy Year pilgrimage from the Archdiocese of Washington, a group of about 230 which I joined as a guest of Archbishop O'Boyle. I was a daily witness to John Spence's managerial skill which went all the way from arranging a papal audience to calming two outraged women who had quarreled in their hotel room in Florence during which one knocked the other to the floor! More than once during those weeks I mused to myself that I was glad it was Spence and not Ellis who had to do the 'directing.' In general, however, Spence carried out his prickly task with genuine success, and the 'pilgrims' were substantially content with his management. And in the years that followed up to his premature death at the age of sixty-four there was many an undertaking that profited from his direction, to name only one, that of Superintendent of Schools of the archdiocese. I left Washington for San Francisco in 1963 and the following year began teaching church history at the University of San Francisco. I cannot now recall what it was that Bishop Spence either read or heard about some of my wayward views on church affairs. I only remember that a few weeks before he died in March, 1973, I had perhaps the only letter he ever wrote me in which in paternal terms he warned against the danger of my being infected with the 'liberal' opinions of certain unnamed Jesuits with whom I was then teaching at USF! What had inspired this counsel, I cannot now recall, if I ever really knew.

Peter Ireton was nearly thirty years older than John Spence. I first came to know him when as Bishop of Richmond he served as a member of the executive committee of the university's Board of Trustees. In that capacity he made repeated visits to the campus when I always found this bluff, stout churchman open, easy of approach, and unvaryingly friendly. As a former Baltimorean he had a keen interest in the biography of James Gibbons which I was then writing. On a visit to Richmond in the summer of 1946 he received the late Henry J. Browne and myself warmly and gave us *carte blanche* in our use of the diocesan archives. It was there that we made ample use of the rich source materials contained in the papers of Denis J. O'Connell, Ireton's predecessor by one remove in the See of Richmond. With the single exception of Baltimore's archives, the O'Connell Papers were the richest deposit of unpublished correspondence I ever encountered in my study of American Catholicism. Harry Browne and I did not discover them, since the Richmond chancellor, Justin D. McClunn, present Vicar General of the Diocese of Arlington, had already done that in two trunks in the attic of the old Richmond chancery; but we were the first professional historians to use them, Harry for his book, *The Catholic Church and the Knights of Labor*, and I for the Gibbons biography. Peter Ireton was a thoroughly likeable man, plain in speech and in manner, a *pater familias* type, who died in April, 1958, at the age of seventy-five.

7

Most Fabulous of All
William Cardinal O'Connell

Let me turn to William Henry O'Connell (1859-1944), whom I have more than once described as the most 'fabulous' Catholic churchman in American history, a man whose personal story, I believe, lends justification to the choice of adjective. I first saw and heard the Cardinal Archbishop of Boston in November, 1928, when as chairman of the Board of Trustees of the Catholic University of America he presided at the installation of the fifth rector, James Hugh Ryan. He was a large man, tall, erect, and very stout. One winter day he was walking along Michigan Avenue opposite the campus in his scarlet biretta and a black cape that enveloped his huge frame. An undergraduate stared across the street and then turned to me and asked, "Who is that?" I told him it was Cardinal O'Connell of Boston, whereupon the student replied, "He looks like a battleship in full sail to me." It was not an altogether inappropriate description of that formidable figure.

The years passed and I only caught a glimpse of O'Connell now and then when he came to the campus for the annual meetings of the hierarchy or the university trustees. Meanwhile I heard more and more stories about the man, more than about any bishop of his own or of a previous generation. If some of these bordered on the incredible, others were so well authenticated by eye witnesses whose testimony was beyond question that they rang true. When Edwin O'Connor's novel, *The Last Hurrah*, appeared in 1956 picturing the feuds between a Boston archbishop and the city's mayor, it was not surprising that many saw here O'Connell and James Michael Curley.

By the time that I was appointed to succeed Monsignor Peter Guilday in teaching American Catholic history I had acquired more than a casual curiosity about the Archbishop of Boston. When, therefore, I decided to spend the second half of the academic year, 1941-1942, at Harvard auditing courses in American social history and utilizing the riches of the Widener Library, I inquired of the priests with whom I was living at Saint Anthony's Rectory in Allston if they thought the cardinal would grant me an audience. They encouraged me to try and the meeting was arranged without difficulty for a March morning in 1942. I was ushered in to the cardinal's office at the chancery in Brighton where I found him seated behind his desk with Moro, his faithful black poodle, resting on the carpet beside him. He greeted me in a friendly manner, holding out his ring to be kissed, and beckoning me to a backless bench in front of his desk. "I understand you have come to study at Harvard," he began, and then told me that they would do all they could to make my stay pleasant, but, he added, "Remember, Father, you are a priest first; do not try to be a Harvard man." I mumbled an assent—dissent was unthinkable in this context—whereupon he inquired if I had read Theodore Maynard's recent book, *The Story of American Catholicism* (1941).

The Maynard book became the principal theme during the next half hour, for I was quickly made aware that His Eminence thoroughly disapproved of the work. He asked if I had read it and when I said I had, he asked, "What do you think of it?" I stated that I thought Maynard had handled two of the most difficult movements in the Church's history in this country rather well. "What were they?" he queried, to which I replied, "Lay trusteeism and Americanism," whereupon there followed an unqualified denunciation of the work. He did not think any of it had been done well. "The book should never have been written," the voice steadily mounting as he warmed to the subject. "Remember," he fairly shouted, "the Church is a sacred thing, she is the bride of Christ, treat her reverently." More than once he stated, "You are in a position to do something about it," which left me non-plussed as to what I was expected to do in the circumstances. For the most part I listened in silence, awed if not a trifle scared, lacking the readiness and wit to say something sensible. I had been scolded for one thing or another a good many times in my life, but I had never experienced anything quite like this. I later learned that the rich metallic voice was frequently heard to grow louder and more menacing the farther O'Connell moved into a topic that had aroused his ire. Incidentally, during the course of the interview Moro got up, came over and sniffed my legs, and returned to lie down beside his master with his little nose cocked high in a way that almost suggested, 'very common clay.' Even the dog bore an air of high disdain!

After about twenty minutes of listening to Cardinal O'Connell's grievances against Theodore Maynard I thought I had heard enough and stated that I did not wish to take any more of his time. "Just a minute, Father, just a minute," he boomed. I realized my blunder too late; he would dismiss me when he had finished; I was not to dismiss myself. After a few more minutes he gave the signal that the meeting had ended, the hand was again held aloft, I was reassured of his willingness to be of any help possible during my stay in Boston, and I departed for Allston to ponder for several days the significance of it all. At the rectory I had a copy of the Maynard book which I took down and searched for the reasons behind the cardinal's chagrin. I am not at all sure that I found them, but Maynard's rather rough treatment of the Irish, I thought, might account for it in part. Another possible cause that occurred to me was Maynard's lengthy chapter entitled, "The Age of Gibbons," with its high praise of Baltimore's first cardinal, whereas the index turned up only a single reference to O'Connell as having attended the International Eucharistic Congress in Chicago in 1926. My interpretation may, indeed, have been too narrow, and Maynard's offense may have been his failure to treat church history from the apologetic approach to which O'Connell was accustomed in earlier writers; if so, it was an approach that was equally unacceptable at that time to most American Catholics.

One of the basic rules for historical narration is to treat persons and events in terms of their own time; nothing less than that is either fair or accurate, and to this rule William O'Connell should be no exception. True, when viewed from the perspective of the 1980's many aspects of his career seem to border on the incredible, and in relating stories about the cardinal I have had people stare at me as though I was making them up for sheer entertainment. His rise to prominence occurred in an age when ultramontanism had achieved most of its goals, and with the death of the relatively benign Leo XIII in 1903 there came the reign of Pius X under whom the centralization of power and the authoritarian temper grew stronger.

To all of this William O'Connell was not only a witness but a zealous participant. During his years as Rector of the North American College at Rome (1895-1901) he formed a close friendship with Raffaele Merry del Val who was one of O'Connell's co-consecrators when he was made a bishop in May, 1901, and sent to govern the Diocese of Portland, Maine. With the advent of Pius X two years later Merry del Val was named Secretary of State, an office in which he wielded tremendous power. For those aware of the

Cardinal William O'Connell

O'Connell-Merry del Val connection it was not surprising, therefore, when the former was named coadjutor to the aging Archbishop John J. Williams in 1906 with the right of succession, the story of which has been told with fascinating detail by James P. Gaffey.[11]

By this time the slowly gathering storm over Modernism had broken. In fact, with the death of Archbishop Williams on August 30, 1907, O'Connell succeeded to the See of Boston just one week before Pius X's encyclical, *Pascendi Dominici gregis*, brought the modernist movement under severe condemnation. If after 1907 there were mild stirrings of the anti-modernist campaign in dioceses like New York, Baltimore, and Rochester, I can think of no such activity relating to Boston. Whatever 'progressive' thoughts may have lingered in the minds of the faculty of Saint John's Seminary, Brighton, after the enlightened rectorship of John B. Hogan, S.S., found no public expression. There is no evidence to suggest, however, that O'Connell—or anyone else—believed that Hogan and his Sulpician successors at Brighton were modernists. If there had been such a concern it would have been removed in 1911 when the cardinal dismissed the Sulpicians in order to inaugurate a Roman model seminary at Saint John's with his own diocesan clergy.

It was in the same year of 1911 that O'Connell was named a cardinal, an event that ushered in the brief period during which his star was in the ascendancy both at Rome and in the United States. It proved to be brief in that the death of Pius X in August, 1914, brought the fall of O'Connell's Roman friend and promoter, Merry del Val, who belonged to the party opposing the new pontiff, Benedict XV. If the Merry del Val connection would tend to have Pope Benedict keep the Archbishop of Boston at a certain distance, that

[11]James P. Gaffey, "The Changing of the Guard: The Rise of Cardinal O'Connell of Boston," *Catholic Historical Review*, LIX (July, 1973), 225-244.

distance was lengthened when the latter's nephew, James O'Connell, chancellor of the archdiocese, left the priesthood, married, and took a substantial sum of archdiocesan funds at his departure. In an audience shortly after World War I, Benedict XV confronted O'Connell with the story, the cardinal denied it, whereupon the pontiff reached into his desk and took out a copy of the marriage license from Crown Point, Indiana, handed it to O'Connell, and the latter dropped to his knees and begged for mercy. The details of this dramatic episode were related to me by my friend and university colleague, Joseph P. Christopher who, in turn, had it from his good friend, Archbishop Filippo Bernardini, first Dean of the School of Canon Law at the Catholic University of America and nephew of Benedict XV's Secretary of State, Cardinal Pietro Gasparri. Gasparri told his nephew that the pope was so indignant at O'Connell's denial that he even thought of removing him from his see. In the event O'Connell remained on in Boston, but for the next quarter century his influence at Rome was reduced to a minimum, even to the extent of being unable to choose his own auxiliary bishops. When, for example, Francis Spellman was named to that post in 1932 it was well known that the appointment was owed to Spellman's close friend, Cardinal Eugenio Pacelli, Secretary of State to Pius XI, and that he was less than welcome to Boston's archbishop. I recall reading in a popular magazine, it may well have been the *Saturday Evening Post*, an article on Spellman which recounted the coolness of his reception in Boston and the citation of a cablegram sent to him when crossing the Atlantic that read, "Congratulations. Confirmations begin Monday."

With the death of Cardinal Gibbons in March, 1921, as the senior American cardinal William O'Connell automatically succeeded to what was then termed the deanship of the national hierarchy. Even his most severe critics could not deny O'Connell's high intelligence, his dedication to what he believed were the Church's best interests, his notable talent as a public speaker, and his superior use of the English language, to say nothing of his cultural tastes and skills as demonstrated in his patronage of fine music and his composition of a number of respectable hymns. In a word, O'Connell's cultivated mind and taste reflected creditably on him and on the Church. He likewise showed a marked talent for administration with the result that the Archdiocese of Boston during his nearly forty years as ordinary was one of the best organized and equipped dioceses in the United States. Moreover, the cardinal was alert to his role as a citizen and spoke frequently and forcefully on public issues, always on the conservative side, however, as shown in his vigorous opposition to such measures as the proposed child labor amendment.

The unquestioned talents of the Cardinal of Boston, however, were flawed by the manner in which he exercised the duties of his high office. The aristocratic bearing had a tendency to put others off, including his fellow bishops, and his occasional outbursts of temper alienated some who might otherwise have been won to his leadership. I recall being told that some years after the publication of the first *Catholic Encyclopedia*, Father John J. Wynne, S.J., one of the original editors, gained permission to address the annual meeting of the bishops in the interests of a new and revised edition. It was said that during Wynne's remarks O'Connell as presiding officer interrupted to say, "Father Wynne, come to the point, come to the point." Thereupon the Bishop of Providence, one of O'Connell's suffragans—it was probably William A. Hickey—rose and declared, "I move that Father Wynne be heard *in extenso*." At that point the cardinal is alleged to have said, "Sit down, Sir, and as long as I am in this chair, do not address it again." The story may have gained in color in the telling, but in any case it illustrated O'Connell's hauteur and less than courteous treatment of a fellow bishop. Incidents of that kind quickly dissolved any attachment that his contemporaries may have felt for the cardinal, and as a result his influence was more and more confined to his own jurisdiction, while the kind of national leadership exercised so successfully by Gibbons vanished to the loss of both Church and State.

Let me mention one final matter in regard to Cardinal O'Connell, namely, his writings. He wrote far more than the ordinary American bishop, a point illustrated by his multi-volume *Sermons and Addresses* that began to appear in 1911 and which extended for a decade or more, a series that touched on numerous current ecclesiastical and national questions. In 1915 the Riverside Press in Cambridge brought out a volume entitled, *The Letters of His Eminence William Cardinal O'Connell Archbishop of Boston*, Volume I, *From College Days 1876 to Bishop of Portland 1901*. It was an attractive book with fine quality paper, gold edged pages, red binding, and numerous illustrations. Many years ago a Boston priest told me the story of the book. He said a review copy was given to a reporter on one of Boston's newspapers and the more he read the more suspicious did he become of its authenticity. Word of his doubts reached the chancery of the archdiocese with the result that my inform-ant's pastor and the cardinal's nephew spent an entire after-noon shoveling copies into the furnace. The letters from "the happy long ago," as the preface read, had been com-posed by O'Connell only a short time before and made to seem that they had been written between 1876 and 1901. When I was doing research for the life of Cardinal Gibbons in the Boston archdiocesan archives I came upon the discol-ored legal size pages in O'Connell's own hand, a somber reminder to an historian of how easily one could be misled as to original source material.

If an inordinate vanity had been the compelling motive for this extraordinary literary effort, the same was not altogether lacking in the cardinal's memoirs, *Recollections of Seventy Years*, published in 1934. Alluding to the 'seventy years' some one is alleged to have wondered aloud how a man born in 1859 could have memories reaching back to the age of five, to which a wag replied, "Children were very precocious in New England in those days." The *Recollections* made entertaining reading a half century ago and sophisticated readers were able to sort out the wheat from the chaff, while the less well informed probably felt carried along by the crescendo of mounting achievements and ecclesiastical honors that marked the Boston cardinal's career. Obviously, William O'Connell's life was one worth writing, but Father John E. Sexton of Saint John's Seminary would have been the first to say that his biography of 1926 written for the cardinal's silver jubilee of episcopacy was not to be taken as scholarly history. Parenthetically, it was with the same Johnny Sexton, as the priests called him, that I lived during my time at Harvard, and it was from this retired professor of church history that I heard some of the most memorable stories about O'Connell. Sexton did not care for the latter and he said he always transacted his business and departed from the ordinary as quickly as possible. Sexton was in a gathering of priests on one occasion during which the cardinal was being taken to task for one thing or another, whereupon Sexton said, "but remember, the bird has brains." Some time later he had to see O'Connell and as he was leaving the latter's parting remark was, "I understand that 'the bird has brains.'" It was an illustration of how directly stories got back to headquarters, although in this case the story, as the Irish say, was by way of no harm.

In the early 1950's O'Connell's successor, Richard J. Cushing, insisted that Dorothy G. Wayman, a convert newspaper woman, write the life of O'Connell and he asked Bishop John J. Wright, his former secretary to assist her. Wright wrote me and asked if I would help Mrs. Wayman which I gladly agreed to do. She told me she felt unequal to the task but showed me correspondence that left little room for escape from Cushing's demands. In due time she finished the work and submitted the manuscript whereupon without her knowledge, as she told me later, substantial changes were made in the text and it appeared in 1955 with a Cushing foreword. Dorothy Wayman was under no illusion about the book, for she was an intelligent woman who had during the course of her research come to know all the untoward affairs in O'Connell's career, including the nephew's departure from the priesthood with all the unhappy details that accompanied that event. To date, unfortunately, there has been no adequate biography of Cardinal O'Connell.[12]

[12]In that connection a highly perceptive essay entitled, "Toward a Biography of Cardinal O'Connell," by Boston's archdiocesan archivist, James M. O'Toole, is awaiting publication in the *Catholic Historical Review*. That essay prompted me to suggest O'Toole as an ideal biographer for Boston's first cardinal, a suggestion to which the then ordinary replied in a polite but non-committal way. I can think of no more suitable person than the same James O'Toole for a serious and scholarly biography of this 'fabulous' controversial churchman.

8

Fulton J. Sheen

One of the prelates with whom I had a close association over a period of years was Fulton J. Sheen. By the time I arrived in Washington in 1927 he was launched upon a career that ultimately brought him international fame as a pulpit orator, a radio preacher, and a brilliant television personality. As a student at Saint Viator College I had heard about him, for he had graduated there in 1917 and was even then regarded as one of the most prominent alumni. In fact, it was through a Saint Viator priest that I was brought to the attention of the young professor at the Catholic University of America. Sheen was looking for a secretary and Father John P. O'Mahoney, C.S.V., on a visit to Washington suggested that he inquire about me since I had served O'Mahoney in that capacity during my college days. Our first meeting was a friendly and informal one and I welcomed the opportunity to earn some money during my years of graduate study. For roughly two years thereafter I would meet Dr. Sheen several times a week in his office in Caldwell Hall when he would dictate letters which I would then type up and deliver to him a few days later.

From the outset I found Fulton Sheen an altogether

agreeable employer. He was unfailingly kind and generous during the time I served as his secretary, a position I felt compelled to relinquish in my final year of graduate work due to the demands of the doctoral dissertation and other duties. I cannot recall any association with him after I left Washington in 1930 until the evening in early June, 1938, when he gave us a conference on the benefit of the holy hour during our retreat for ordination. It was that evening that he asked if I would live with him upon my return in the fall when I was scheduled to begin full-time teaching at the university. He was intent on having the Blessed Sacrament reserved in his home, and for that privilege it was then necessary to have several priests living together.

Such was the background for my moving into the Sheen residence in the 4500 block of Cathedral Avenue in north-west Washington in September, 1938, where I resided, along with Father Lucian Lauerman and several other priests who lived with us for brief periods of time. It was an arrangement that lasted until the summer of 1941 when Monsignor Sheen sold the house preparatory to building a new residence off Foxhall Road. He invited me to live in the new residence, but I told him that I had decided to move to the campus, since I had grown weary of the six-mile drive each class day and, too, I found it rather lonely due to his frequent absences from home. I told several close friends that repeated weekends with the English setter and the canary as my sole companions were not sufficient compensation for the privilege of residing in the fashionable capital neighborhood of Wesley Heights! Sheen said he understood and we parted company in good spirits.

By 1941 Sheen's fame was well established and he was on his way to further honors and achievements. I observed, however, that while fully conscious of his rising star he never permitted his enhanced status to overtake his consideration for those with whom he lived. For example, if a subject arose on which we differed he would almost immediately drop it rather than to insist on having his own view prevail. Moreover, I have rarely known a more generous person, for with his increasing income his charities mounted in due proportion. This characteristic was notably true in his checking out in a single week the $65,000—I believe that was the amount—he inherited from the estate of the papal duchess, Genevieve Garvan Brady MacCauley, most of which went to benefactions to black Catholics in the Diocese of Mobile.

One of the most pleasant recollections I have of my time on Cathedral Avenue was the devoted service of Mrs. Fanny Washington, the black housekeeper and excellent cook, toward whom Fulton always showed a touching sensitivity. The final story I heard about Fanny concerned her former employer's sending an automobile from New York to bring her to Saint Patrick's Cathedral where he received her into the Catholic Church after he had become National Director of the Society for the Propagation of the Faith in 1950. It was typical of his treatment of this splendid Christian woman, as it was of others who served him such as his faithful secretary, Margaret Yates. And while speaking of the monsignor's generosity I should not omit mention of what he told me in 1956 when I asked him if it was true that he had sent to the Roman headquarters of the Propagation of the Faith $26,000,000 the previous year. He replied, "$24,600,000 of which one million was my personal contribution," the latter being income from his telecast programs.

No one can live under the same roof with another person for three years without coming to know the latter fairly well. We were never what one might call close friends, even if our relationship was never other than cordial. I never thought of him in the same category as Ed Cardinal, for example, and I am certain he never thought of me in that way. I admired his priestliness—I was a witness to his daily Mass and holy hour, to name only two features of his prayer life—and I was impressed as well by his steady work habits, his reading, his love and zeal for the Church and, as I have said, his genuine thoughtfulness for those around him of whatever station in life. The single flaw that at times became tiresome was Fulton Sheen's vanity. For example, in preparation for delivery the following Sunday he began to read me his sermons at table. I soon found this less than engaging, so I determined I would try to stop the practice in as tactful a manner as I knew how. One day I brought a book of poems to lunch and asked if he would tell me which one he thought most appropriate to end a sermon I was then preparing. It worked. We never had another 'reading lesson' at meals.

By the late 1930's Monsignor Sheen had become a national figure, and when Cardinal Patrick Hayes died suddenly in September, 1938, the media began mentioning Sheen's name as a possible successor. I think this might be cited as an instance where Sheen's vanity betrayed him, for he took the newspaper reports with a seriousness that they distinctly did not deserve. If I had been unaware of just how seriously he had regarded these speculations, I was made unmistakably conscious of his deep disappointment when in April, 1939, Pope Pius XII appointed Francis J. Spellman as Archbishop of New York. I was at lunch with him on the day of the announcement and I vividly recall his depressed state of mind. Leaning his arm on the table with his head in his hand, he exclaimed, "It is incredible. It is incredible. He has nothing." So deeply dejected was he that he took to his bed and remained there for several days. It was sad to see so gifted a man led astray by the utterly uninformed reports of newsmen and perhaps of equally uninformed ardent admirers of the nation's stellar Catholic pulpit orator. In a lesser degree a similar occurrence took place when some years later rumors began to circulate that he was to be made a cardinal. In that connection I recall his asking me to give him the titles of biographies of cardinals when I visited him in New York in the summer of 1956.

By that time Fulton Sheen had been a bishop for five

Archbishop Fulton J. Sheen

years and had made a remarkable success of his office with
the Society for the Propagation of the Faith to which he had
been appointed in 1950 in large measure through the influence of Cardinal Spellman. Meanwhile, however, the two
men had fallen out over control of the Society's finances,
and an abyss had been fixed between them that was never
bridged. After Sheen's departure from Washington I occasionally visited him in New York, and I recall the day in
July, 1956, when I called at his office and was greeted with
an altogether unaccustomed warmth and invited to dinner.
The Spellman feud had lowered his spirits and he obviously
needed someone to whom he could speak freely. I listened
that evening for about three hours during dinner at the
Waldorf Astoria and a walk down Park Avenue. The details
were colorful and in certain respects rather grim. One of the
final items of which I have memory was his pointing to the
Church of Our Saviour at 38th Street and Park Avenue as
he remarked, "I was appointed pastor of that church," an

appointment from Cardinal Spellman which, he made clear, he had declined. I later wondered if he might have regretted declining that appointment when in 1966 he was named Bishop of Rochester by Pope Paul VI—I would presume again at the instance of Spellman—an assignment which he in no sense welcomed and from which he resigned after three years of a rather stormy and unhappy regime in northwestern New York.

Bishop Sheen dearly loved New York and when he retired from Rochester he returned to live there, Cardinal Spellman having died two years before. I recall that when Cardinal Mundelein died in October, 1939, Sheen's name once again began to circulate in the press for Chicago, but he showed not the slightest interest in that prospect. When I came in from class that January morning of 1940 and told him that there was a new Archbishop of Chicago, Samuel Stritch of Milwaukee, he manifested complete indifference. Mention New York and the big expressive eyes gleamed; mention Chicago and they revealed something akin to boredom.

The contribution of Archbishop Sheen—he was named a titular archbishop in 1969—to the Catholic Church and to the general American public was incalculable. Countless men and women, and the young as well, were spiritually enriched by his extraordinary preaching, numerous converts to Catholicism found peace of mind by his instruction, and thousands of Americans of every religious faith and of none called his name blessed. His forte was the pulpit and the public platform whether it be the lecture forum, the radio, and in later years the television screen. His written message as embodied in his many books was less satisfying. Personally, I often followed his spoken discourses with rapt attention, but I confess I found his books uninteresting due to a fault that may well have been my own rather than his. The final volume, the posthumously published memoirs, *Treasure in Clay. The Autobiography of Fulton J. Sheen* (1980) was a distinct disappointment to me as an historian of American Catholicism. For me an air of unreality pervaded its pages and, of course, the magic of the voice and vibrant personality that had held thousands enthralled through over a half century were missing.

When Fulton Sheen died in December, 1979, at the age of eighty-four it was altogether appropriate that his final resting place should have been the burial vault beneath the high altar of New York's Saint Patrick's Cathedral, for the pulpit of that historic church had never been so frequently and so uniquely adorned as it had by the twentieth century's most famous Catholic preacher. Several years ago I asked to be shown the cathedral burial vault, and as I stood gazing at the tombs of Cardinal Spellman and Archbishop Sheen, the last two up to that time to be buried there, I thought of the transitory character of this life when measured against the background of eternity. The circumstances of the lives of these two churchmen's last years brought to mind the final statement of Saint Thomas More at Westminster Hall on that July day of 1535 when he addressed his judges and prayed that, "...though your lordships have now here in earth been judges to my condemnation, we may hereafter in heaven merrily all meet together, to our everlasting salvation."[13] May the same be true of Fulton Sheen and Francis Spellman.

[13]E. E. Reynolds (Ed.), *The Heart of Thomas More. Readings for Every Day of the Year.* Springfield, Illinois: Templegate. 1966. p. 93.

Cardinal Spellman and Company

The diary kept during my first trip to Europe in the summer of 1931 recorded that on the evening of August 9 I first laid eyes on Francis Spellman in the lobby of the Hotel Continental in Paris. As I passed the unknown clergyman said 'good evening,' recognizing, I suppose, a fellow American when he saw one. I had not the faintest idea of who he was, but when I reached the room of Fulton Sheen, who had invited me to dinner, he asked if I had seen an American priest in the lobby. "That," he said, "was Monsignor Spellman of Boston who has flown in from Rome with Pius XI's encyclical, *Non Abbiamo Bisogno*, against Mussolini to release it to the world press." Only later did I realize the full significance of that action in the mounting feud between Pius XI and Il Duce. It was a year before Spellman was named Auxiliary Bishop of Boston, and I doubt that at the time I so much as knew his name. The time ahead, however, was to bring that name forward in a way that imprinted it on the Church's history as no other American name since that of Cardinal Gibbons.

A decade passed and I remember no occasion when I came in contact with the Archbishop of New York, a post to which, as I have said, he was appointed in April, 1939. My introduction to him came in November, 1941, when his Roman classmate and my friend, John Cartwright, invited me to ride with them to Baltimore for the sesquicentennial of the American Sulpicians. Another classmate of theirs, Joe Christopher, sat in the middle of the back seat with the archbishop on one side and myself on the other. As the junior member of the company I kept silent. About half way Spellman leaned around Chris and asked, "Father Ellis, to what diocese do you belong?" It happened that still another Roman classmate, Julius Haun, was a priest of the Diocese of Winona to which I then belonged, a good but somewhat eccentric man. When I answered 'Winona,' 'Spelly,' a name he used himself among his intimate friends, emitted a quiet chuckle and remarked, "Bishop Kelly (then ordinary of Winona), Julius Haun, and Father Ellis." It was my first experience of that curious gurgle that sounded something like a giggle, a sound that left one perplexed as to whether he was laughing at you or with you. After several more questions in my direction the conversation between the Roman classmates resumed as we neared Baltimore where the Fifth Regiment Armory and Saint Mary's Seminary, Roland Park, were the scenes of the memorable celebration of the Sulpicians' 150 years of service to the American Church.

It was frequently said that two men of that generation had an extraordinary gift for remembering people's names, Archbishop Spellman and James A. Farley, Postmaster General in the cabinet of President Franklin Roosevelt. I could testify that it was true of the former. After our first meeting in November, 1941, I do not recall having seen him again at close range for probably two years. I was going along the corridor of Caldwell Hall one day on my way to lunch when I came upon the Archbishop of New York in conversation with Bishop Joseph Schlarman of Peoria. As I passed the archbishop turned and said, "Hello, Father Ellis." I was frankly astonished at the time that he should have remembered my name, but I learned that this was something that was habitual with him.

At the close of one of the annual meetings of the American Catholic Historical Association in New York in the early 1940's—we met there three times between 1940 and 1946—my friend, Ed Cardinal, and I found ourselves with nothing much to do on New Year's Day so we decided to attend the archbishop's reception. Immediately behind us was the same James Farley mentioned above. Suddenly Bishop James Francis McIntyre crossed the room, handed Farley a letter, and exclaimed, "What are we going to do with these people?" If I overheard the identity of 'these people' at the time, I cannot now remember who they were. In any case, the annoyed bishop received a reply which, I suspect, was something less than satisfactory when the astute Farley quietly answered, "I am afraid, Bishop, that the situation will grow worse before it grows any better," or words to that effect. By this time Ed and I had reached the archbishop who after taking a quick glance at us looked behind at Farley and said, "Here are two historians, Jim. They can tell us what happened last week but they can't tell us what will happen next week." Spelly could not be gainsaid on that one!

My next meeting with Archbishop Spellman came in the spring of 1945. The previous year he had engaged the lay historian, Thomas F. O'Connor, to write the biography of New York's first archbishop, John Hughes. Simply as a matter of course I wrote a note for the January issue of the *Catholic Historical Review*. Early one morning I received a call that Archbishop Spellman wished to see me in Curley Hall. Upon arrival I found him in the company of the executive committee of the university trustees. He started off by a mild reprimand for my having published the news about the O'Connor appointment. As near as I can at present recall his words the statement went something like this: "You should not have published that. I was the one to make known the appointment." I said I was sorry to have overlooked that fact, whereupon he quickly made it clear that the rebuke was not to be taken too seriously and proceeded to the matter then uppermost in his mind. Parenthetically, I later learned that a scolding followed by a reassuring remark was a fairly common practice in Spellman's dealings with people.

The archbishop's concern on this occasion had to do with the lack of progress of the Hughes biography and his desire that Tom O'Connor be made aware of that fact. Would I speak to the latter? I agreed to do so, although I could not promise success. Tom was a thoroughly competent historian, but his periodic drinking bouts slowed him down and often rendered him incapable of work. Later that day I sought him out—he was then living in the university neighborhood—upbraided him sternly and told him his job was in jeopardy. I found my mission a painful one, for Tom was a lovable person for whom I had not only professional respect but affection. He promised to shape up and get back to work, but the trouble lingered on and in 1948 came the parting of the ways and Tom returned to Saint Louis University where he taught up to his sudden death in September, 1950, at the age of fifty-one.

Meanwhile Cardinal Spellman asked Henry J. Browne, then a priest of the Archdiocese of New York, archivist of the Catholic University of America and a member of the Department of History, to undertake the biography of Hughes. I recall vividly the high enthusiasm with which he began the work and the professional skill with which he brought off nine chapters all of which I read at Harry's request. These were sent to the cardinal as they were completed, only to elicit mostly negative reactions, such as "Monsignor So and So does not like it." When I think of the surprising candor about Spellman's early career which appeared with his approval in the first chapters of Robert I. Gannon's *The Cardinal Spellman Story* (1962), I regret that

Harry Browne's chapters were not read and judged by the cardinal himself instead of being turned over to 'critics' whose concept of church history was nothing less than "sweetness and light" in all that pertained to the lives of churchmen, a *modus operandi* that no self-respecting historian could or would accept. The failure of Harry Browne's work to be completed—he once told me five chapters remained to be written—and published was a distinct loss to American Catholic historiography. We have traveled a considerable distance in that regard since the days of the ill-fated biography of John Hughes, although church history as a vehicle of apologetics is still cherished by a dwindling number of conservative clergymen.

Cardinal Spellman came to the campus from time to time, for example, to meetings of the Board of Trustees or for ecclesiastical events in the National Shrine of the Immaculate Conception. I remember being told by the master of ceremonies, Walter J. Schmitz, S.S., that on one of these occasions in the Shrine when Spellman was scheduled to preach, Wally offered to put the manuscript on the lectern. "Oh, no you won't," said Spelly, "If I lose this we will have three Our Fathers and three Hail Marys." He had the winning characteristic of now and then laughing at himself. He was quite unimpressive in the pulpit or on the public platform, something which, I think, he recognized and, therefore, he frequently engaged Fulton Sheen *et al.*, to speak in his own cathedral when he might have been expected to preach himself.

My next contact with the Cardinal of New York came in 1952 as a result of my trip that summer through South America. A little background is necessary by way of the *mise en scène*, as the French say. I was asked to make the trip by the Department of State, the reason being, as Edward G. Miller, Assistant Secretary for Latin American affairs, informed me, that most Latin Americans considered us Americans to be 'Protestants and materialists.' It was thought that if I as a Catholic priest and university professor would visit there and give lectures on Catholicism in this country, meet the leading churchmen and educators, etc., it might prove helpful. In each capital I called on the local ordinary, the nuncio, and several of the prominent Catholic educators. All in all, I was very courteously received, and especially was that true in Lima and Santiago. In Peru the nuncio, Archbishop Giovanni Panico, went out of his way to be friendly, and in Santiago the archbishop, José Maria Caro, Chile's first cardinal, who spoke English fairly well, had me to lunch during which we had a delightful visit. He was a generally beloved figure as I heard on all sides. I remember telling him that he reminded me of pictures of Cardinal Gibbons, whereupon he quietly replied, "That is because I am so old." The aged churchman's mental alertness belied his eighty-six years. I should add here that in Lima the Maryknoll Fathers were most hospitable, as was true in Santiago of the American Holy Cross Fathers at Saint George's College.

The intellectual and religious climate in South America was then quite different from that of our day. The current friendly relations of Catholics and Protestants was at that time non-existent, and everywhere I went I was met with protests in Catholic circles about American Protestant missionaries. The first complaint on that score was in Bogotà where the nuncio, Archbishop Antonio Samoré, brought up the subject in a mild way, as did the Cardinal Archbishop of Santiago a week or so later. Polite remonstrances gave way, however, in Rio de Janeiro where the nuncio, Archbishop Carlo Chiarlo, was anything but mild on the subject. On my first visit to the nunciature in the then capital of Brazil, Monsignor Giovanni Ferrofino, then the auditor, was kind and informative, as he was at dinner at the Hotel Gloria to which I invited him one evening. I remarked to Ferrofino that I had gathered the impression that the cardinals of these Latin American capital cities did not count for much, to which I received the rather puzzling reply, "The Cardinal of Lima is nothing, the Cardinal of Buenos Aires is nothing. The last consistory was a political consistory." I confess that from that day to this I never quite figured out just what Ferrofino meant.

On my second visit to the nunciature with the wonderfully kind American cultural attaché in Rio de Janeiro, my historian friend, Thomas E. Downey, Ferrofino received us with his customary warmth. As for the nuncio, I will let my diary entry for July 27, 1952, tell the tale. I wrote:

> Archbishop Chiarlo came down looking very much like an unfriendly bulldog and acting in the same manner for most of our stay. His conduct was very close to rudeness—e.g., scolding at Americans for their hasty visits to South America to establish 'contacts,' at the coming of American Protestant missionaries here etc. He thawed out only very little before we left and when I went to kiss his ring he snatched his hand away as though I were going to bite it!

It was this unpleasant encounter that I found so outrageous I felt, perhaps naively, should be reported to someone who might do something about it. After my return home I wrote Spellman and stated that I was to be in New York with my mother later that month and would like to tell him of a certain experience I had in Brazil. During breakfast at our hotel some weeks later I was called to the telephone and informed by his secretary that the cardinal would like to have mother and me to lunch that day.

There were a half dozen other guests at the luncheon table, including Robert I. Gannon, S.J., former President of Fordham University, who had been asked by the cardinal to write his life. As it turned out I had no chance beyond a few hasty sentences to tell Spellman what I had in mind, since by that time Spelly's mind was quite fixed on something else. I had just completed the life of Cardinal Gibbons and he thought I might be of help to Gannon. If my effort to bring action in regard to Chiarlo failed, so too did Spellman's attempt to enlist my aid in the writing of his own biography. A letter written shortly thereafter to Gannon did not so much as elicit a reply.

After lunch the cardinal asked one of his attendants to show me his library of clippings on the second floor, a collection which from a superficial examination seemed an impressive one and which, I presume, is now housed among the Spellman Papers at Saint Joseph's Seminary in Yonkers. When I came down stairs I found the cardinal in the parlor seated next to my mother with whom he was chatting away and to whom, as we prepared to leave, he gave an autographed copy of his prayer book, a large volume bound in red which she cherished until her death in 1955. Whatever the unproductive outcome about the anti-American sentiments of Archbishop Chiarlo, I at least had first hand evidence of how offhand and casual Francis Spellman could be and, needless to say, I was especially touched by his warm reception of my mother who often regaled her friends in Seneca about her lunch with the famous cardinal.

Cardinal Spellman

No one of national prominence in Church or State can escape criticism. Francis Spellman's strong stands on public issues such as birth control, movie censorship, American diplomatic relations with the Holy See, public aid to private schools, and the war in Viet Nam guaranteed that it would be true in his regard. On most questions the cardinal held his ground in the face of strenuous opposition, for example, in his defense of the American presence in Viet Nam. At other times the strength of his championing a cause would vary with changing circumstances. I now recall only one case when he made open overtures to an adversary, and that was in his controversy of 1949 with Eleanor Roosevelt on the score of public financial assistance to private religious schools. In this instance he went to Canossa, so to speak, when he called on Mrs. Roosevelt at Hyde Park in an effort to make peace. Exactly what motivated him on that occasion, I frankly do not know, but I do know that long after James A. Farley, Roosevelt's former postmaster general, told me at one of our several meetings in New York, that in an audience of Pope Pius XII the latter had expressed his disapproval of Spellman's attack on Mrs. Roosevelt. It would not be unlikely that word of the pope's displeasure should have been conveyed to Spellman and that may, indeed, have been behind his trip to Hyde Park. In any case, a peace of sorts was patched up between the principals to the dispute without either having yielded his or her basic view.

Cardinal Spellman's sudden death on December 2, 1967, may with plausibility be said to have ended an era in American Catholic history, coming as it did so soon after the close of Vatican Council II. In matters theological he had no special training, and his intensely practical approach to life and its problems kept speculative questions mostly at a distance. His natural instincts prompted him in the main to espouse the traditional way of doing things that he had always known. Yet he was not at all a reactionary, and when the council's liturgical changes, which he had steadily opposed, were enacted he gave word that they were to be immediately implemented in his archdiocese. He fully shared with his fellow bishops from the United States a deep conviction about the need for the Church to adopt the principle of religious freedom. Thus when he learned that conservative influences had kept John Courtney Murray, S.J., the outstanding theologian on that question, from the council's first session he promptly saw to it that Murray was brought to Rome under his personal auspices.

The Cardinal of New York was not only keenly aware of the implications of the axiom, *sentire cum ecclesia*, but he was normally a practioner of that principle. Yet his was no slavish adherence to the will of distant Roman authorities, as Monsignor Giovanni Baptista Montini, the future Paul VI, found out on one occasion when he criticized American policies and was stoutly taken to task by the Archbishop of New York. The incident is fully described by Gerald P. Fogarty, S.J., of the University of Virginia in his recent scholarly work, *The Vatican and the American Hierarchy from 1870 to 1965* (1982), a volume wherein Spellman emerges as the commanding American churchman in the years after 1940.

Whoever undertakes to write the life of New York's fourth cardinal archbishop—and it certainly should be written, and that before all who knew him have departed—will have to grapple with a very complex character. I have frequently heard Spellman dismissed as an ambitious careerist, Rome's errand boy, as it were, a mediocrity who through cultivating powerful people had risen far beyond his true merits. That he cultivated the high and mighty in Church and State, there is no doubt, a fact candidly admitted in a biography he himself approved. That he was unimpressive in appearance, in public address, and in his general presence was also true. Yet beneath the commonplace exterior there were qualities of a superior order, for example, high administrative talent, shrewdness to a marked degree, sharp intelligence in practical matters, all of which were employed in a dedication to the Church that was never in question. Without wishing to indulge in the dramatic, I would say that Cardinal Spellman was the kind of man who would have given his life for the Church if circumstances had called for it. If his novel, *The Foundling* (1951), and his poetry have earned no lasting place in American literature, and if his infrequent excursions that touched upon theology were never taken with the seriousness of those of his contemporary, Cardinal Emmanuel Suhard, Archbishop of Paris, it would be a gross injustice to maintain that in the final analysis his contribution was other than positive, allowing, to be sure, for the mistakes and errors that are the lot of us all.

I should like at this point to say something about several other bishops who were associated at one period or another with Francis Spellman. In that category I think of Bonaventure F. Broderick, James Francis McIntyre, and Richard J. Cushing. I first met Broderick on Easter Sunday of 1942. I had come down from Harvard to New York for the Easter holidays, and after offering Mass at Saint Patrick's Cathedral one of the staff asked me if I would serve as Broderick's chaplain for the high Mass about to be offered by Archbishop Spellman. I can still see Spelly looking quizzically across at Broderick and me as we chatted while waiting for the procession to move, as if to say, 'What, I wonder, are those two talking about?'

Bonaventure Broderick had had an unusual career about which I learned in due time. After having served for several years with the papal representative in Havana, Cuba, this Connecticut-born priest had been named auxiliary bishop there in 1903, a time when tension between Washington and Havana was still a reality in the aftermath of the Spanish-American War. I never knew exactly why, but for some reason Broderick became *persona non grata* in Havana and was removed in 1905. Thereupon the papal Secretary of

State, Merry del Val, suggested to Cardinal Gibbons that Broderick be named the Holy See's agent for the collection of Peter's Pence in the United States. The Cardinal of Baltimore responded with unaccustomed firmness in vetoing the suggestion as a reflection on the generosity of the American Catholics toward Rome; moreover, Broderick, he said, would not be welcome in the national capital.

In the sequel the bishop was set adrift to fend for himself without a definite appointment or adequate income. This condition obtained for roughly thirty years and ultimately ended by his working in a gas station in Millbrook, a small town above New York City. Upon Spellman's arrival in New York in 1939 the Broderick case was brought to his attention by Amleto Cicognani, the apostolic delegate, with the result that the archbishop moved quietly and without delay. He interviewed Broderick at the latter's place of employment, learned of his good disposition toward the Church, restored him to his rightful ecclesiastical status, and appointed him as archdiocesan vicar for religious with residence at the Frances Schervier Home for the aged.

During our conversation at the cathedral the bishop invited me to dinner at his residence where he showed me certain memorabilia and discoursed at some length about certain aspects of his life without, however, alluding to the precise details of his time in Havana. What he did make unmistakably clear that evening was his disapproval of Cardinal Gibbons who, he said, was a vain man who did not want any 'purple' about him lest monsignori detract from his own place in the spotlight. At the time I knew relatively little about Gibbons and, therefore, for the most part listened in silence. Later I became aware that in regard to the cardinal's alleged vanity he did show that characteristic in such things as liking ecclesiastical processions in which he would figure in his cardinalitial robes. But I also learned that the charge that he would have no purple-clad monsignori around him was not true, for he had as many of these as was the custom at that time in most American dioceses. It was understandable in view of Gibbons' attitude toward Broderick many years before that the latter should harbor some negative memories. It is pleasant to record that when the strange career of Bonaventure Broderick came to an end in November, 1943, at the age of seventy-five, Spellman saw to it that he was accorded all the honors that befitted his episcopal rank.

Long before that New Year's Day in the early 1940's when I first laid eyes on James Francis McIntyre at the Spellman reception, I had heard much about this handsome and impressive looking prelate, especially from my dear friend, John P. Monaghan, pastor of Saint Michael's Church in west 34th Street. I found the stories of their frequent confrontations highly amusing told, as they were, with my friend's inimitable flair. John was one of the principal founders of the Association of Catholic Trade Unionists as well as being identified with other progressive groups that aroused the suspicions of the conservative bishop with his Wall Street background. On one occasion in the midst of an argument at the chancery McIntyre exclaimed, "John, you are shouting," to which Monaghan countered, "Bishop, you are shouting," and with that exchange the temperature dropped a degree or two.

Yet if McIntyre was notoriously short-tempered and often prone to angry outbursts about matters on which he was less than well informed, there was another side to his character. That side I heard more than once from Fulton Sheen who considered him a deeply spiritual man to whom he went regularly to confession. Fulton told me that when Bishop James Griffiths, a New York auxiliary, refused to hear the confession of Fulton's recent convert, Clare Boothe Luce, unless she would issue a public statement concerning her marital status, he turned to McIntyre who heard the famous lady's confession with no conditions attached. I learned of this side of McIntyre's character from others as well, for example, my historian friend, Tom O'Connor. When McIntyre was made a bishop in 1940 no one was louder in praise of the appointment than the same Fulton Sheen. Thus as in the case of so many others there was here a mixed picture of dark spots which, of course, received the publicity, while the sympathetic actions toward those in trouble went unnoticed such, for example, as personally taking night calls from skid row in Los Angeles during his years as archbishop there.

My first personal meeting with James Francis McIntyre took place in the summer of 1960 while I was teaching at Mount Saint Mary's College in Los Angeles. He had been named second archbishop there in 1948 and in 1953 created a cardinal by Pius XII. The general assumption that he owed his promotion to Spellman was confirmed some time later when the late Monsignor Thomas McCarthy told me that one day walking up Madison Avenue in New York with Spelly the latter remarked, "There is an axis in the Middle

Cardinal McIntyre

West working against me (he was referring to Mooney of Detroit, Stritch of Chicago, and McNicholas of Cincinnati), so I thought I would make my own axis." The story has about it the ring of truth, for Spellman had come to have a high regard for McIntyre. At the time of the latter's appointment as a bishop, Sheen remarked to me that he had congratulated Spellman, who stated that he had sought the appointment while fully aware that McIntrye had not wanted him in New York as successor to Cardinal Hayes.

Of the Spellman-McIntyre close ties, then, there was no doubt. Yet the Archbishop of Los Angeles remained his own man for all that. For example, when the Soviet leader, Nikita Khrushchev, was scheduled to visit the United States in 1959, the White House was at pains to make known its uneasiness lest the American cardinals should spark an outcry against the Russian premier's presence. Eisenhower's Undersecretary of State, Robert Murphy, was sent to New York to intercede with Spellman in that regard. The latter told Murphy that since Cushing of Boston had already spoken it was too late in that quarter. He assured him that Cardinal John O'Hara of Philadelphia would say nothing, and he then added, "As for Los Angeles, you had better speak to him yourself." Knowing McIntyre's passionate dislike of Communism and the tenacity with which he maintained views about which he felt strongly, the Cardinal of New York was simply being realistic about an approach of that kind to his former coadjutor.

During my stay in Los Angeles in that summer of 1960 I was invited to dinner at Saint Gregory's Rectory by the pastor, Timothy Manning, then one of McIntyre's auxiliary bishops who in 1970 was named his successor. He inquired if I had seen the cardinal, to which I replied I had not and added facetiously, "Is it safe?" As a result of Bishop Manning's suggestion I wrote McIntyre and received a prompt and cordial invitation to lunch at his residence in Fremont Place. I was accompanied by the late Father James O'Reilly, then a professor at Mount Saint Mary's, and Monsignor Benjamin Hawkes, secretary to the cardinal, made the fourth at table.

I recall that McIntyre and Hawkes had recently seen "My Fair Lady" and were as enthralled as the rest of us by that sparkling musical comedy. The most serious topic of conversation, as I now remember it, was the cardinal's impatience with the tardy pace of the *New Catholic Encyclopedia*. He quizzed me closely about the reasons for the delay, to which I could give no really satisfactory answers since I had resigned as editor for the historical articles on American Catholicism having lost confidence in the editor-in-chief's ability and intention to produce a work of genuine scholarship. I later contributed four or five articles at the urging of my good friend, Martin R.P. McGuire, who played a major role in bringing the undertaking to completion. All in all it was a very pleasant luncheon after which Cardinal McIntyre invited me to walk with him in the garden. As we strolled up and down he inquired about various persons and happenings in the East, with special mention of his New York seminary classmate, Patrick O'Boyle, Archbishop of Washington, to whom he referred familiarly as 'Rick.'

An interval of four years elapsed before I again met the Archbishop of Los Angeles. I was quickly made aware that the friendly attitude of our 1960 meeting had meanwhile vanished and that McIntyre now viewed me in an entirely different light. The circumstances were as follows. In May of 1964 Mount Angel Abbey some miles south of Portland, Oregon, celebrated its diamond jubilee. I was asked to preach the sermon at the Mass at which Cardinal McIntrye presided. The latter must have quickly given signals of his displeasure at what I had said, for I was greeted by knowing smiles and remarks by several of the prelates present as we lined up for the group picture in front of the abbey church. I was not aware of any untoward reaction until Thomas A.

Connolly, then Archbishop of Seattle, and Leo T. Maher, then Bishop of Santa Rosa, gave unmistakable signs of trouble ahead. I remember saying to the latter, "Do you think I should call the police?" It was only after the picture-taking that I learned from Father Ambrose Zenner, O.S.B., rector of the seminary, that the cardinal was greatly upset by what he thought I had said. "He thinks," said Zenner, "that you said we have a lot to learn from Karl Barth about how to run our seminaries. He would like to see your manuscript." I readily handed over the latter to him and he took it to McIntyre who, he later told me, paged through it with mounting fury trying to discover the offending passages. Actually, I had quoted Barth as having said the Protestants had a lot more to learn from the Roman Catholics than many Protestants realized. The cardinal's hearing had become somewhat impaired and that probably accounted for the mistaken impression in part. Yet I still believe that stories of my involvement in the fuss that arose at the university in 1963 over the rector's having denied four outstanding theologians an opportunity to lecture at the students' invitation, was the real reason for the attitude revealed at Mount Angel. I had become involved, as I have said, in that controversy by telling an editor of a Catholic newspaper that things of that kind had been happening at the university for a decade or more. The remark received wide publicity and brought upon me the wrath of a number of ecclesiastics, including the university's chancellor, Archbishop O'Boyle, and the former rector, Bryan J. McEntegart, both of whom were friends of the Cardinal of Los Angeles.

Be that as it may, the storm broke into the open at the Mount Angel celebration during the luncheon that followed the Mass. Cardinal McIntyre was among the speakers and after congratulating the Benedictines on their diamond jubilee he turned to what was uppermost in his mind. "I would disagree," he exclaimed, "with the speaker of this morning.

He is introducing dubious novelties, whereas I think we should stay with the old, the tried, and the true." As he warmed to the subject his high pitched voice rose in indignation to the point where the audience of four archbishops, four bishops, and four abbots along with roughly 200 priests were more alert than they had probably been at any luncheon address in many a day. When he finished the guests rose and applauded. I could hardly do otherwise myself incongruous as it must have appeared for one to applaud his own denunciation.

Following the Cardinal of Los Angeles came James P. Davis, then Archbishop of Santa Fe, who complimented the monks on their jubilee and then remarked, "I disagree with the previous speaker. I would agree with everything the preacher said this morning." The sharp disagreement of the two archbishops amused the audience and there was a good deal of laughter among the guests. After the luncheon I thanked Archbishop Davis and said he had been brave, indeed, to which he replied, "I am not brave, John, I am only foolish." I have no doubt that forty-eight hours after the event there would not have been more than a handful among those present who could have recounted what I had said in the sermon, for that is the fate, alas, of most sermons. But as I remarked to my friends, if they may have forgotten the sermon, the Benedictines of Mount Angel and their guests would certainly not soon forget their diamond jubilee day! As I was going up the stairs from the dining room Cardinal McIntyre was just ahead of me. I reach out my hand and said "good-by," a salutation that was greeted by a hasty handshake and a frown. It was my final meeting with the formidable churchman about whom, as I have said, I had heard much over the years from John Monaghan and others. As I now ponder that memorable day in Oregon I think of the glee with which Monaghan would have witnessed the encounter between me and his ofttime sparring partner in the heyday of ACTU and other Catholic movements of the left.

Cardinal O'Hara

Before turning to Cardinal Cooke, who succeeded Spellman, I should like to make a few remarks about another Spellman associate and close collaborator, namely John O'Hara, C.S.C., who died in 1960 as Cardinal Archbishop of Philadelphia. One of my earliest impressions of O'Hara came from his confrère, the late Thomas T. McAvoy, C.S.C., of the University of Notre Dame. Tom and I met on board a New York Central train one evening in late December, 1951, on our way to the annual meeting of the historians. I asked if he was going to Philadelphia the following month for O'Hara's installation as archbishop. "No," he answered, "there are some of us (meaning the Holy Cross Fathers) who do not care for him. You know when he was president of Notre Dame he used to spend his noon hour in the library tearing up books, especially those on the reserve shelf of Father Ray Murray in sociology." Between Tom's notorious mumbling manner of speech and the noise of the train I simply could not believe what I was hearing, so

I asked, "Did you say destroying books?" "Yes," said Mc-
Avoy, "tearing them up." For me the exchange came close
to a high water mark for anti-intellectualism in Catholic
academia. Parenthetically, among those often puzzled by
Tom's mumbling was the same John Monaghan to whose
Saint Michael's Church McAvoy would frequently go to
offer Mass upon arriving in New York. One day, so
Monaghan told me, during breakfast Tom's mumbling
became particularly frustrating to his host who later said, "I
knew Ellis was catching hell but I could not make out
precisely what Tom was saying."

Curiously, in 1967 McAvoy published a highly detailed
biography of Cardinal O'Hara in which he cited numerous
critics of the Philadelphia archbishop without adding any
criticisms of his own. It was in that work that I came upon
an oblique reference to myself that made it clear I was on
O'Hara's condemned list. My curiosity was piqued and I
asked Cardinal John Krol, O'Hara's successor, if I might
have access to the Philadelphia archives, a permission which
he readily granted. Through the kind assistance of Monsignor Arthur J. Nace of the chancery staff the pertinent
documents were placed at my disposal. Spellman had written O'Hara to inquire if he knew what had prompted a
recent *monitum* from the Holy See about the open criticism
of certain Catholics concerning matters relating to the
Church in this country. O'Hara told his New York friend
that in his judgment the Roman letter had been inspired by
"those blatherskites, Hesburgh, Weigel, and Ellis." I felt I
was in good company when named with Notre Dame's
famous president and the distinguished Jesuit theologian,
even though I was sorry to have pained the Cardinal of
Philadelphia. The latter was a genuinely pious man who, I
am sure, was highly motivated and accomplished much
good, but his rigidly conservative nature could not abide
airing of weaknesses in the Catholic community, especially
by priests. That was in all likelihood the reason why meeting

him early one morning at Notre Dame my "good morning" was greeted only by an icy stare.

•

When the publisher asked if I would add to this memoir some remarks concerning the recently deceased Cardinal Archbishop of New York, there came to mind Saint Paul's words about the Lord's stewards. "What is expected of stewards," said the apostle, "is that each one should be found worthy of his trust." (*I Corinthians*, 4:2). If any single message came through during the last days and death of Terence Cooke, the public reaction, it seemed to me, was that here, indeed, had been a churchman 'found worthy of his trust.'

I first met the late cardinal c. 1949 at the university in Washington when he was a graduate student in social work. At no time did I know him well, but I would meet him at infrequent intervals in the sacristy of Saint Patrick's Cathedral when I would go there to offer mass. He was invariably friendly, as he was to all with whom he came in contact, a characteristic that would account, I believe, for the repeated mention following his death on October 6, 1983, of the word 'kindly,' perhaps the most frequently used word to be found in the tributes and comments spoken about him.

The only explanation I ever heard for his choice as the successor of Cardinal Spellman was that the latter had requested his appointment by the Holy See before his own death. That there were close ties between the two, there is no doubt, a fact attested by Cooke's steady advancement from secretary to Spellman in 1957 to his appointment as auxiliary bishop in 1965. That Cooke retained a deep attachment to his predecessor was well known, and as he came near to the end of his prolonged illness I heard more than one person remark that his death would signal 'the end of the Spellman regime.' There probably was some truth to this, although the two men were vastly different in their attitude toward the world around them. Francis Spellman thoroughly enjoyed being in the spotlight, while Terence Cooke seemed to make a studied effort to avoid the public gaze. In spite of their differences of temperament and style, however, the bond between the two was, as I have said, a very close one.

I had reason to perceive this in the spring of 1970. The occasion was the meeting of the hierarchy in Detroit when the chairmen of the sub-committees for the National Conference of Catholic Bishops' study of the American priesthood reported to the bishops at their semi-annual gathering. In my remarks as chairman of the sub-committee on history I stated that it had been a heartening experience for many of us when Cardinal Spellman, learning that John Courtney Murray had been excluded from the opening session of Vatican Council II, appointed the distinguished theologian to come to the council as his personal *peritus*. Following my talk I happened to meet Cardinal Cooke in the corridor when he stopped me and expressed profuse thanks for my mention of the episode. It was obvious that he had been more gratified by my remarks about Spellman than by anything else I had said.

I went to Rome in October, 1974, as scholar-in-residence at the North American College and visiting professor of church history in the Gregorian University. During my year and a half there the Cardinal of New York would come from time to time on business at the Holy See during which he was a guest of the College. We would meet at the social hour and at dinner where he was always friendly and attentive to those in the company, for example, asking me one evening if I would say grace before dinner because, I suppose, I was the senior in age among the dozen or so at the table. To be sure, it was a small matter, but it was a succession of these small matters that added up to a widespread impression of a thoughtful person whose high ecclesiastical rank had not been allowed to distance him from those of a lesser station in life.

It was at Rome at this time that I met Edwin F. O'Brien, a New York priest studying for his doctorate in moral theology at the Angelicum. Ed and I became good friends, and as a consequence after he came to reside at the cathedral rectory in New York I was frequently there as his guest. I was in New York for Christmas of 1978 and on Christmas Eve the cardinal and his secretaries came to dinner at the cathedral rectory. During dinner I inquired of Monsignor James F. Rigney, rector of the cathedral, how the project for a volume marking the cathedral's centennial was coming along. He made clear that it was to be in large measure a picture book rather than a real history. Cardinal Cooke overheard my question and after dinner he called me aside in the rector's apartment and asked if I would help in securing an historian for a scholarly history of Saint Patrick's. I told him I would be glad to be of assistance, but I would first like to inquire if the person chosen would have full access to the sources and, secondly, if that person would be free to write the story in an objective way that would allow for the telling of untoward events should the latter prove necessary for a complete account of the cathedral's story. I was assured on both points that the author would be permitted to proceed in a truly professional fashion.

In the sequel I submitted several names of prospective authors, and Sister Margaret Carthy, O.S.U., of the College of New Rochelle, author of three scholarly works in church history and editor for American Catholicism for the *New Catholic Encyclopedia*, was chosen. She experienced no difficulty on the score of official censorship of what she wrote, even if the treatment accorded her at the archdiocesan archives left much to be desired. When completed the manuscript was quickly accepted for publication by Michael Glazier, Inc., and is published under the title *A Cathedral of Suitable Magnificence: The Story of St. Patrick's Cathedral in New York* with a foreword bearing the signature of Cardinal Cooke.

It would not be in accordance with reality to portray Terence Cooke as a great leader in the sense of electrifying the masses by his actions or by his spoken or written words. If I have caught the true measure of the man, I would say that he sensed he had not the extraordinary ability to influence and impress the public mind with the sagacity and charm of a Cardinal Gibbons nor the eloquence and charism in public address of an Archbishop Sheen. He always impressed me as one who knew his limitations, accepted them, and sought to serve others on a plane where he was comfortable and assured with no pretensions to a style of leadership which to him would be unreal.

Cardinal Cooke was a gentle man in whose conduct there was reflected a deep courtesy which is of the essence of true love and charity toward one's fellow human beings. In that regard I think of Hilaire Belloc's little poem of which Terence Cooke was a true exemplar. Belloc wrote:

> Of Courtesy, it is much less
> Than Courage of Heart or Holiness
> Yet in my walks it seems to me
> That the Grace of God is in Courtesy.

It is, indeed, and the late Cardinal of New York showed that quality even when those of lesser moral stature would have laid aside courtesy in the face of public insult, for example, when the cardinal calmly accepted without rebuke the insulting conduct of a young Jesuit at an ordination ceremony at Fordham University.

As I write these lines the body of Cardinal Cooke is being laid away in the crypt beneath the high altar of his cathedral. I have been influenced no doubt by the tributes paid to this churchman in recent days and, too, by his final pastoral letters to his own flock and to Irish Americans in particular to whom he wrote less than a week before he died:

> At this time of my life, I make a special plea to you. I make it from the depths of my soul. There have been circumstances

which have caused misunderstandings and division among us,
and I ask you now to work with all your hearts for healing, for
reconciliation and for an end to violence here in our own
community and in Ireland.[14]

They were fitting last words from a dying archbishop, and
they blended well with the cardinal's strenuous efforts
against the scourge of abortion and other anti-life movements in which he took a conspicuous part. So, too, were his
final messages to the 1,840,000 Catholics of the New York
archdiocese and the 2,125,000 American Catholics whom
Terence Cooke served in his capacity as vicar of the Military
Vicariate, a separate jurisdiction for the men and women in
the armed forces and their families stationed throughout the
world.

There were, to be sure, critics of Cardinal Cooke, as there
were of Cardinal Medeiros of Boston. That is among the
inevitable accompaniments of the lives of those highly
placed in either Church or State. Yet the scenes that marked
the deaths and burials of the two cardinals attested to the
sincere regard in which thousands of their respective flocks
held them, for example, the eleven Masses in Boston
between Humberto Medeiros' death and burial when literally thousands of the 1,925,000 Catholics of the Archdiocese
of Boston left scarcely more than standing room at these
memorial Masses. The same was true of the throngs that
passed the bier of Terence Cooke in the cathedral on Fifth
Avenue during the days before his funeral. These manifesta-
tions say something, surely, of the spiritual and moral leadership exercised by these two churchmen. The quiet lines of
people moving slowly in and out of the cathedrals of Boston
and New York in those days spoke eloquently of a type of
leadership which touches the human heart in ways that no
historian can record, for it lies hidden in the souls of men

[14]*Catholic New York*, October 6, 1983, p. 24.

and women who recognized in a Humberto Medeiros and a Terence Cooke an influence that transcends the visible world and finds its focus in a world beyond. And for whatever may have been left undone at their passing the two cardinals might rightly appropriate the words of John Henry Newman when he declared:

> One alone among the sons of men has carried out a perfect work, and satisfied and exhausted the mission on which He came. One alone has with His last breath said 'Consummatum est.' But all who set about their duties in faith and hope and love, with a resolute heart and a devoted will, are able, weak though they be, to do what, though incomplete, is imperishable.[15]

[15] John Henry Newman, *The Idea of a University*. Edited with introduction and notes by Ian T. Ker. Oxford: At the Clarendon Press. 1976. p. 224.

Red Hats in Boston and Saint Louis

What a vastly different person was Richard Cushing! My original meeting with him had its amusing aspects. It was November, 1945, and the bishops were in Washington for their annual assembly which in those days was still held on the campus of the university. I had begun the research on the life of Cardinal Gibbons the previous summer and I was anxious to interview John J. Glennon, Archbishop of Saint Louis, who had preached the eulogy at Gibbons' funeral. Glennon was then in his eighty-fourth year having ruled in Saint Louis for forty-two years. In the midst of our interview there appeared at the door of the room in Caldwell Hall the tall figure of Boston's new archbishop. "Archbishop," he called out, "can you tell me how to get to 1312 Massachusetts Avenue?" (the headquarters of the National Catholic Welfare Conference). Glennon gazed around the room and up at the ceiling and quietly replied, "Well, it is not here." At that point I interjected to give Cushing directions as best I could, whereupon he wheeled about and strode down the corridor. "Who was that?" asked Glennon. I told him it was the Archbishop of Boston, which drew the terse comment, "A young looking man, isn't he?" I would have given a penny that day to know Cushing's thoughts about the patriarch from the Middle West; I saw only the puzzled glance and the swift departure back to the world of reality.

In the belief that a memoir allows a certain amount of literary license, so to speak, I am going to inject at this point some recollections about my meeting with Cardinal Glennon before treating Boston's third archbishop. I had been introduced to the Archbishop of Saint Louis the previous evening after dinner in Curley Hall by Edward B. Jordan, vice rector of the university. The old man was cordiality itself, asking me at the outset about my own background. Upon hearing that I had been born in the Diocese of Peoria, he smiled broadly and asked, "Why don't you write the life of the Bishop of Peoria?" (Joseph H. Schlarman). While I do not know what I answered, I do remember well that Schlarman was not on Glennon's list of favored persons. "Did you ever see him?" he asked. Yes, I said, I had seen him *en passant* but had never met him. And then with a gesture and a mimicking air he declared, "He is statuesque."

During the interview the following day I became aware that Glennon had entered upon a state of euphoria not uncommon with old people and that his memory was playing tricks on him. For example, I asked how it came about that he was the preacher at Gibbons' funeral since I was not aware, I said, that they had been closely associated. He answered, "It was that coadjutor in Baltimore who invited me. Is he still living?" First, Owen Corrigan was Gibbons' auxiliary bishop, not coadjutor, and he had been dead for sixteen years. *Caute*, I said to myself. The archbishop went on to recount the circumstances of his first meeting with Gibbons when the latter was passing through Kansas City in 1894 to the installation of Placide L. Chapelle as Archbishop of Santa Fe. Glennon was then auxiliary bishop and was sent to the railroad station to welcome Gibbons and his traveling companions. "I brought him a little of that that is good to have when one is traveling," he remarked. It was a homely little detail, even if it did not add much to my knowledge of his relations to the man whose life I was writing.

Upon the termination of the interview I volunteered to walk Archbishop Glennon back to Curley Hall. Seeing a stout clergyman approaching us, he asked me, "Who is this?" I answered, "He is Bishop William Mulloy of Covington." By this time Mulloy was abreast of us and he greeted Glennon with great effusion. "So you are from Covington," the old man began and then added, "I preached in your cathedral once." "Oh, did you, Your Grace," replied Mulloy in a tone of high enthusiasm. The archbishop's next remark, however—which incidentally he repeated twice—brought no more than a stunned silence. "I shall always remember it," said Glennon, "they had a little nigger dressed in green to carry my train." I later learned of his dislike of blacks, but this was stark evidence, indeed.

When one recalls that Glennon's predecessor by one remove, Peter Richard Kenrick, had held similar views and had ruled the Archdiocese of Saint Louis from 1843 to 1895, it was not surprising that Glennon's successor, Joseph E. Ritter, should have encountered stiff opposition from many Catholics in 1946 when he inaugurated a policy of racial integration, a resistance that compelled him to resort to the threat of excommunication. Kenrick's fifty-two years, plus Glennon's forty-three, added up to nearly a century of official unfriendliness, a heritage which took Archbishop Ritter time and struggle to overcome. At the time of our meeting Glennon reminded me that he would be the third bishop in the history of the American Church to reach the golden jubilee of his episcopacy, "that is, if you people will leave me alone." I assured him that we would 'leave him alone,' and would welcome this extraordinary anniversary which would match that of Kenrick in 1891 and Gibbons in 1918. In the sequel he was named Saint Louis' first cardinal in February, 1946, but he died in Dublin on his way home from the consistory less than four months short of his golden episcopal jubilee.

I now return to Glennon's 'young man' to whom I first spoke in November, 1945. Richard Cushing was then fifty years of age having completed one year as Archbishop of Boston, a tall angular figure whose gravely voice, familiar address, casual manner, and common touch were during the next quarter century to make an indelible impression on Americans of every walk of life. If those who were responsible for his appointment had set out to select one who would offer a striking contrast to Cardinal O'Connell, whose auxiliary bishop he had been for five years, they could not have improved on the choice. When I recall the propriety and sedateness of Amleto Cicognani, Apostolic Delegate at the time, I find it difficult to picture him as the one who furthered Cushing's promotion. I do not pretend to know the real situation, but I should not be surprised if future historians with access to the documents would discover that the controlling hand had been that of Cushing's fellow-Bostonian, Francis Spellman, with whom he had formerly worked closely. Cushing had become known for his extraordinary ability to raise money for the Church, a talent that made his name a byword during his long tenure of the office of archdiocesan Director of the Society for the Propagation of the Faith, and that in Catholic circles both in this country and in Rome.

If in 1944, therefore, he was a relative stranger to most Americans, he was known as a conspicuous success to the Society's world headquarters. That fact would not have left his former Boston associate, the Archbishop of New York, unimpressed, for Spelly was nothing if not alert and practical in such matters as raising money for ecclesiastical purposes. By this time it was obvious that Spellman's star was in the ascendant with his close friend, Pius XII, occupying the chair of Peter, and it would be altogether natural that the pontiff would have consulted Spellman before filling the latter's native diocese. Let that suffice for speculation about how Richard Cushing became Boston's third archbishop.

From time to time Archbishop Cushing was invited to speak in Washington and I would see and hear him on those occasions. His sermons and public addresses were generally well prepared and contained real substance, although they were often unconscionably long as, for example, his sermon in the National Shrine of the Immaculate Conception at the Mass commemorating Saint Anthony of Padua as a doctor of the Church on a beastly hot day in the summer of 1946, when Cushing preached for nigh to an hour. Nor will I ever forget a Pan American Mass at Saint Patrick's Church when Cushing, by now a cardinal, occupied the throne while Archbishop O'Boyle sat on a faldstool in the center of the sanctuary facing the congregation. Once in the pulpit that inimitable voice began thus: "Your Excellency, the Most Reverend Apostolic Delegate, Your Excellency, the Chief Justice of the United States," along with a half dozen other names of notables in attendance. When he finished the personal salutations he called out, "Now if I have omitted anybody you will have to blame Archbishop O'Boyle because he gave me this list to read." It was probably an uncomfortable moment for the Archbishop of Washington, although it afforded the rest of us a hilarious interval amid the liturgical solemnities.

Whether or not Richard Cushing wrote his public addresses, I do not know. I suspect that in his first years as archbishop they may have been written by John J. Wright, his auxiliary bishop, whose fertile mind was more than capable of such an assignment. I know that when the American Catholic Historical Association was preparing to hold its annual meeting in Boston in Christmas Week of 1949, as secretary I invited Cushing to speak at our presidential luncheon. He promptly accepted and soon thereafter I received a letter from Wright in which he equivalently asked, 'What do you wish him to say'? I thereupon drew up a rough draft or outline of the need for a broader and deeper study of the history of the Church. At the luncheon at the Hotel Statler on December 30 Richard held forth with great eloquence on that theme much to the edification of the historians gathered for the occasion. In all likelihood few Americans who heard the Archbishop of Boston's prayer at the inauguration of President John F. Kennedy that snowy day in January, 1961, will now recall a word he said, but they will not have forgotten its length, to say nothing of the podium catching fire and causing a momentary stir. It was the kind of situation that Richard Cushing thoroughly enjoyed.

I met Cardinal Cushing briefly—he was named to the Sacred College in December, 1958—in March, 1967, when I was asked to give the address at the dedication of the new library of Saint John's Seminary, Brighton. But he was not well that day that saw New England's heaviest snowfall of the year, and he departed for the big house on the hill immediately after the blessing of the building. By this time I had come to know the gruff churchman well after our several weeks together at the North American College in Rome where he was present for the final session of Vatican Council II and I for a series of lectures to the students at the invitation of the rector, Bishop Francis F. Reh. I was placed next to him at table and across from Cardinal Ritter of Saint Louis with their *periti* and the faculty making up the pleasant company.

It did not take me long to catch on that Cushing loved to stunt and to amuse the assembly, a situation that I found entirely congenial; thus I believe I can say that we 'hit it off' well from the outset. One day someone remarked that he found Cardinal Spellman's Latin rather difficult, whereupon Richard turned to me and said, "I find his English rather difficult." On another occasion one of the men stated that he thought Fulton Sheen looked very young, to which another replied, "He is only sixty-five." I interposed at that

Cardinal Cushing

point to say that I had lived with him for three years and knew that he had turned seventy the previous May. Then with mischievous intent I turned to the Cardinal of Boston and said, "He is just about three months older than you are, Eminence, is he not?" At that he boomed out, "Yeah, but don't connect me with that guy!"

After only a few weeks Cushing announced that he was going home. I expressed surprise and remonstrated with him that he should remain until the close of the council. Once he had delivered his strong intervention in behalf of religious freedom, however, and spoken in favor of the statement on the Jews, he manifested little interest in the proceedings. "I can't understand what they're saying," he exclaimed with his customary candor, a confession with which I had real sympathy, for I was understanding relatively little myself of the debates in the *aula*. He maintained that he could do more for the Church at home than he could at the council, probably alluding to his extraordinary success in raising money, a talent that at the time was still evident, although it tapered off near the end of his life.

One evening before the cardinal's departure I was walking along the corridor on my way to the dining room when the elevator opened, out he stepped, and without further ado called out, "Do you want to meet the pope?" When I said I would be happy to do so Cushing replied, "Well, be ready at six o'clock tomorrow night." In the interval I scurried around to find the proper attire—in those days one did not go to a papal audience with the informality that some do today—borrowed a monsignor's robes, and off that evening Richard and I went to the Vatican. As it turned out, we were about a dozen in number, all Bostonians except myself. Upon our arrival Cushing first entered the pope's study alone and after a few minutes he emerged and beckoned us to come forward. Since I was the sole non-Bostonian I held back a bit, only to have Pope Paul VI gesture to me to come forward with the words, "The professor." Cushing had apparently briefed the pontiff on our identity, and the latter had remembered that there was a professor in the group. In any case, I stepped forward and had my picture taken with the pope, the cardinal, and several of Boston's archdiocesan officials, a memento I have kept through the years.

Like Newman's gentleman, Paul VI had his eyes on all his company, asking us questions and giving to each a rosary, a medal, or some token gift. He appeared rather fatigued, as well he may have been at the end of a long day of work and appointments of one kind or another. It was my second so-called private audience, having previously been received by Pius XII at the instance of Romolo Carboni, whom I had known during his time at the Delegation in Washington and who since 1969 has been Apostolic Nuncio to Italy.

Needless to say, I was aware of certain failings and weaknesses of Richard Cushing, an inheritance that he shared with all the rest of us. For example, his generosity at times outran his purse and he gave out money when the supply was dangerously close to exhaustion. In that connection I am reminded of an amusing story told to me by my historian friend, John B. McGloin, S.J., of the University of San Francisco. One of John's sisters was a member of the Religious of the Secred Heart who conducted a girl's college in Montevideo. She came to the United States to raise funds for the institution, was sent by her brother to me for suggestions, and I mentioned certain likely people from whom she might hope to gain assistance, among them Cardinal Cushing. John told me later that she received an appointment and was waiting in a room of the Boston chancery when she heard Cushing call out in a loud tone meant for her to hear, "There is some nun here from Latin America. Well, she won't get anything from me." Entering the room he said, "Well, Sister, what can I do for you?" Upon stating that she would like to explain their work in Latin America, she was cut short by the remark, "I don't give a damn about Latin America." Mother Genevieve McGloin had her wits about her that day, for she immediately retorted, "I don't give a damn either, Your Eminence, but I am giving my life for this cause." She had struck precisely the right note, for he declared, "Good for you, Sister, I'll give you $100,000." I asked my Jesuit friend if his sister ever got it, and he said that she did, indeed, in installments of $10,000 at a time. Timidity on that occasion would not have impressed the big fellow, but Mother McGloin's forthright reply immediately won him and the benefaction was not only promised but ultimately delivered. I suspect that many another could have told a similar tale, and that particularly in Latin America where Cushing's Society of Saint James did such splendid work under his munificent patronage.

The years after Vatican Council II were all pretty much down hill for the Cardinal of Boston. The mid- and late-1960's ushered in a new era for the American Catholic community, a time when old certainties gave way to doubts and challenges in the form of student demonstrations, departures from the priesthood and religious life, and deep divisiveness that destroyed the erstwhile calm and orderliness of individual parishes. For a churchman like Richard Cushing accustomed to an hierarchial rule that was seldom challenged and rarely openly disobeyed, the change was beyond his ability to cope with to say nothing of controlling. In fact, there was a serious disruption at his own Saint John's Seminary, Brighton, on one occasion that taxed the ailing cardinal's strength and shook his confidence. What made the situation all the more painful was that he had lost his onetime robust health with serious respiratory trouble and ultimately contracted cancer that sapped his vitality.

My final meeting with Cardinal Cushing in the autumn of 1969 was a sad one. I had an engagement to speak to the priests of the Diocese of Manchester and had written ahead to my friend, Monsignor John A. Broderick, then rector of the seminary, to say that if he thought well of it I would call on the cardinal to pay my respects before flying back to San

Francisco. John answered, "He needs to see a friendly face," and we went, therefore, to the cardinal's residence in advance of my flight. I found the once buoyant and happy churchman I had known at Rome a saddened and depressed man. He made no effort to conceal his state of mind, and that especially in regard to so many priests leaving the ministry. "Do you understand it?" he asked. I confessed that I did not and added that I found it something of a mystery. I tried as best I could to lift his spirits, but the effort was pretty much in vain. After about a half hour I remarked that I would have to leave for the airport, whereupon he rose and began to weep, holding my hand and saying, "I have a great affection for you, John." I was deeply touched and knelt and asked for his blessing with tears in my eyes, assuring him of my own affection for him, a sentiment that I could express with complete sincerity.

That final meeting took place almost a year to the day of his death on the feast of All Souls of 1970, less than a month after the installation of his successor, Humberto Medeiros, a ceremony at which, I was delighted to hear, Richard Cushing received a thunderous ovation from the vast throng in attendance. It was an entirely deserved and fitting farewell to a prelate who had given the best that was in him to Church and State through his life of seventy-five years.

Cardinal Cushing was not alone among his episcopal colleagues in finding the post-conciliar Church a trying experience. Accustomed as they were to a generally docile and obedient flock of priests, religious, and laity, the new mood of questioning authority, public demonstrations of dissent, and in certain cases noisy and angry exits from the priesthood and religious life, to say nothing of the rising rate of divorce and remarriage among many lay persons, made the bishops' lot an unenviable one. Historians will probably feature the open opposition to Paul VI's encyclical, *Humanae vitae*, of July, 1968, as a high water mark in that regard. Yet 15 years later the spirit of extreme individualism often characterized as 'looking out for number one,' still pervades a portion of the Catholic community.

Amid all the turmoil that divisive issues have continued to cause, the bishops have reacted in a variety of ways, for example, from the relatively calm and reasoned manner in which Cardinal Lawrence Shehan handled the crisis over the birth control encyclical in the Archdiocese of Baltimore to the resignation of the See of Portland, Oregon, by Robert Dwyer at the age of 65, a deeply disillusioned man who had, so to speak, given up the struggle. In between a Shehan and a Dwyer there were bishops who rode the revolutionary wave in a way that won the hearts of most of their people, men such as Paul Hallinan, Archbishop of Atlanta, about whom I will have something to say in what follows.

In showing varying reactions to contemporary difficulties bishops are no different than the rest of us, in that some are endowed with the qualities needed in what Newman once called "an uncertain, anxious time," while others not so endowed have found the post-conciliar years a trial beyond their capacity to cope. Here, I have often thought, bishops—again like the rest of us—can find both reassurance and comfort in the history of their kind in earlier ages. If a bishop of the 1980's is tempted to discouragement, let him read an account of his episcopal forebears in the 980's in such a work as Nicholas Cheetham's *Keepers of the Keys* (1983) and he will, I believe, take heart in the realization that 1,000 years ago a bishop's lot was infinitely worse than his own.

When I think of the career of Cardinal Cushing's former auxiliary bishop, John J. Wright (1909-1979), I hope and pray that he did not destroy his papers as, alas, Cushing did to the grave loss of American Catholic history. Had I even so much as an inkling of his intention in that regard I would have pleaded strongly with him, for I believe he would not have resented my doing so. But whether it would have done any good is very doubtful, for he seemed to attach no importance at all to the preservation of such papers. In that connection I think of the paper on which he had jotted down the names of the principal *papabili* in the conclave of 1963 that had elected Paul VI. He showed it briefly to Monsignor Francis J. Lally that June 21 and then quickly put it back in the sleeve of his cassock. Frank took in some of the leading names and that evening while dining with Cardinal Gregory Agagianian mentioned several of the front-runners among whom was the Armenian cardinal himself. Frank told me that Agagianian at first gave a startled glance, asked how he had known these names, and then smiled knowingly and said, "Who but Cardinal Cushing!" I suspect that the document ultimately ended in pieces in the wastebasket of Richard's room at the North American College. If so, his violation of the secrecy governing the conclave's proceedings was only a slight one.

These two closely associated Bostonians, Cushing and Wright, were a striking contrast in every respect. The former was the big gruff fellow from South Boston's Irish enclave, generous almost to a fault with little of what the sophisticated would call polish. Wright, on the contrary, was highly literate, widely read, and urbane, a graduate of the Boston Latin School among the alumni of which he moved with ease, a company in which Cushing would not have felt at home. Yet in spite of their differences they seemed to work well together during the years before Wright went off to Worcester in 1950 as the first ordinary of that new diocese. What their relations were thereafter, I do not know, but a Boston priest friend told me that on the day of Cushing's death Wright, by this time a curial cardinal at Rome, was in the Kennedy International Airport in New York ready to fly for the Eternal City and he telephoned to Boston to say that he would preach the funeral sermon. The late cardinal would probably have been as content with Wright's eulogy as with that of any other.

Although I met John Wright only at infrequent intervals

our relations were invariably friendly. If after the mid 1960's when he became increasingly critical of many post-conciliar developments in the Church I felt I could not share some of his views, our earlier relationship found us much more closely allied. For example, he reacted with genuine enthusiasm to my controversial essay, *American Catholics and the Intellectual Life*, and when it was published in book form in 1956 he contributed a lengthy foreword which he entitled "Prefatory Note" in which he strongly championed my central thesis that the Catholics of the United States had not contributed anywhere near what their numbers, improved economic status, and educational level would warrant. With his customary wit and wisdom the then Bishop of Worcester seconded my viewpoint, noted that most of the written reactions had thus far sustained my approach, but stated there was no reason to believe that all the reactions had been thus far registered. "One awaits with mingled sentiments of dread and curiosity," said Wright, "this season's commencement addresses, for example!" John Wright's stocks were then very high in Catholic academic circles, and I was gratified, therefore, to have his support, especially in view of the opinions of certain members of the hierarchy who were anything but pleased with that essay. In fact, one archbishop whom I happened to meet shortly after its publication alluded to the fuss it had caused and then remarked, "You had better let the subject alone for a while."

I have already mentioned my correspondence with Bishop Wright concerning the Wayman biography of William Henry O'Connell and Richard Cushing's luncheon address to the historians at Boston in 1949. From time to time I heard from him again, for example, when he very generously nominated me to membership in the American Academy of Arts and Sciences and asked me to accept if the invitation came my way; in fact, it never did. Meanwhile Wright was named Bishop of Pittsburgh in 1959, and the single memory I have of his days in western Pennsylvania was the night that he came to give the address to the departing deacon class at the Theological College of the Catholic University of America. I cannot recall specifically what he talked about, but I do remember that he had the audience in one outburst of laughter after another. He was at times hilariously witty and that night we laughed as one seldom does at gatherings of that kind. On occasion Wright's wit could be costly as, for example, when he referred at Rome to his *alma mater*, the North American College, whose current policies he did not approve, as "the American zoo." The big house on the Janiculum was not amused!

In his very informative volume, *American Participation in the Second Vatican Council* (1967), Monsignor Vincent A. Yzermans stated that as a member of the theological commission Bishop Wright made thirty-two trips to Rome and attended about 240 meetings of that group. When later asked what he thought had been the commission's most satisfying achievements, he began his answer in a vein of

Cardinal Wright

thought that is worth quoting. "I am convinced," he said,

> that the Church is faced, as is the world, with the long 'winter'
> that must follow the rise of atheistic humanism and 'technolo-
> gism.' It is a chapter of history foretold by prophetic spirits:
> Newman, Soloviev, among many...[16]

In the time that has passed since the close of the council in
1965 the Church has, indeed, experienced a 'long winter,'
and that not alone from the forces of atheistic humanism
but as well from the debilitating divisiveness within her own
membership, an aftermath that accompanied more than one
ecumenical council in her history.

During Vatican Council II John Wright played a relatively minor role in the debates, as was likewise true of that
other highly visible and articulate American, Fulton Sheen.
In that regard Wright's most distinctive contribution cen-
tered on the role of the laity, a subject to which he warmed as
in his intervention of October 17, 1963, when he stated:

> In truth, I can say that the Christian faithful have been
> waiting four hundred years for such a positive conciliar exposi-
> tion, such as is now presented by the Council, on the place,
> dignity and vocation of the laity in the Church of Christ.[17]

That emphasis, often reiterated, endeared him to the
Catholic laity among whom Wright's name was probably
held in greater esteem than was true among many of his
fellow clergymen.

In 1969 the Bishop of Pittsburgh was named a cardinal *in
curia* and appointed Prefect of the Congregation for the
Clergy. This new and final chapter of his life proved to be
one of the less happy periods of his seventy years in this
world. For one thing, he was plagued by ill health which
steadily worsened to the point that the crippling arthritis

[16]Vincent A. Yzermans (Ed.), *American Participation in the Second Vatican
Council.* New York: Sheed and Ward. 1967. p. 21.
[17]*Ibid.*, p. 62.

and circulatory problems not only slowed down his movement but at times kept him stationary for extended periods. When I went to Rome as scholar-in-residence at the North American College and visiting professor of church history at the Gregorian University in October, 1974, he was still able to get about, and on Thanksgiving Day he came to the Casa Santa Maria in the Via dell' Umiltà where he celebrated the Mass and preached. As the procession moved into the chapel he spied me, left the line of march, embraced me with a vigorous hug, and welcomed me to Rome. Some weeks later he invited me to dinner at his apartment near the Vatican when, I remember, we spoke at length of Newman, of Cardinal O'Connell, and others about whom he had a rich vein of recollection that was expressed in his blend of stately diction and keen wit that proved not only entertaining but informative.

Before I left Rome the following June I invited the cardinal, his secretary, Father Donald Wuerl, and several priests from the Casa Santa Maria among whom was Father William J. Fay of the Diocese of Pittsburgh to lunch. Once he had been comfortably seated—he moved that day with great difficulty—he held forth in his accustomed fashion with one story after another. The only interruption that I can remember was the appearance of Archbishop Agostino Casaroli, now Secretary of State to Pope John Paul II, who stopped to pay his respects to the American cardinal.

Our luncheon party on that Sunday in the spring of 1975 was the last time I saw Cardinal Wright. When I returned to Rome in January, 1976, for my final semester of teaching— this at the Angelicum—his health had deteriorated rather seriously and he was confined pretty much to his apartment with less and less time at his office. That doubtless had something to do with his state of mind, for he had grown increasingly conservative in his outlook and more critical of those who, he felt, had contributed to the Church's malaise by their lack of discipline and their adoption of attitudes and conduct at variance with the traditional ways to which he had been accustomed. Inevitably, those of a different turn of mind reacted to Wright's barbs and as a consequence his reputation in clerical circles was damaged. Once again, there was a certain parallel here to the final years of Archbishop Sheen who, as I was told by one who was present, stated on his departure from the Diocese of Rochester, "My greatest cross has been you priests." It was a sad fact in the final years of both men, for it would be difficult to think of two more talented prelates of their generation than the same John Wright and Fulton Sheen.

I have made passing reference in these recollections to Joseph E. Ritter, the unassuming man who ruled the Archdiocese of Indianapolis for twelve years before being appointed in 1946 as Archbishop of Saint Louis. If he was unassuming and quiet spoken, he was in no sense lacking in courage as he proved when he initiated a policy of racial integration and took strong measures to enforce it on those Saint Louis Catholics who opposed him. That struggle became a *cause célèbre* that projected Ritter into a national spotlight he had not previously known.

I came to know the archbishop in circumstances much less dramatic than the fight for racial justice. Although not a trained historian, he had a keen interest in the history of the American Church. While in Indianapolis he had sent a priest to the Catholic University of America to be trained by Peter Guilday with the thought that he would then write the history of the archdiocese. The man in question took the Ph.D. degree in 1939, but at his death in 1964 the work remained unfinished. The same thing happened in Saint Louis where Ritter chose a priest to get the doctorate, which he did in 1953 with a fine study relating to the Catholic Indian missions. In the latter case, however, the priest was seriously hampered by diabetes which explained in part that at his death in 1975 there was no archdiocesan history. When the historians' annual meeting convened in Saint Louis in 1956

Archbishop Ritter presided at the luncheon conference and thereafter quizzed me closely about the unfinished history. I could only plead ignorance of the matter for I had heard nothing about it since the prospective author had left Washington.

In the final letter I had from Cardinal Ritter a few weeks before his death he went over the story of his unhappy experiences in Indianapolis and Saint Louis in this regard. He mentioned at that time that Saint Louis might finally have found its Catholic historian in William Barnaby Faherty, S.J., of Saint Louis University. It is pleasant to record that the cardinal's hope was ultimately fulfilled in a highly creditable way with the publication in 1973 of Father Faherty's volume, *Dream by the River. Two Centuries of Saint Louis Catholicism, 1766-1967*, which, unfortunately, the cardinal did not live to see. I have gone into some detail on this subject to show that the failure of church history has not always been due to the lack of interest and support from the bishops, a charge we historians have at times unfairly made. In certain instances it has been Clio's disciples who must bear the blame.

My closest acquaintance with Saint Louis' second cardinal came during Vatican Council II when, as I have said, I was at table with him at the North American College. I found him an altogether agreeable person with whom I had a number of friendly chats, a man who impressed me as utterly unpretentious and approachable, one who knew his own mind and was not afraid to express it both in private conversation and in strong interventions in the conciliar debates. In that connection the index of the Yzermans volume reveals no American bishop, except Cardinals Spellman and Albert Meyer, with more interventions than the Cardinal of Saint Louis. One day after lunch Ritter and I were the only ones left in the dining room. How the name of the recently appointed Archbishop of Chicago, John P. Cody, came up, I cannot now recall; but I did not forget the quiet comment that came across the table from the man under whom Cody's episcopal career began as auxiliary bishop. Ritter simply stated, "John Cody will take care of John Cody." It was only later that the significance of the remark struck me when the Chicago ecclesiastical scene began to darken under the same John Cody.

At the approach of the golden jubilee of Cardinal Ritter's priesthood I wrote him my congratulations and recalled our happy days at Rome two years before. In a reply dated May 17, 1967, he thanked me, rehearsed as I have mentioned, the account of the unwritten histories and his anticipation of William Faherty's work. He closed by saying, "Be assured, dear Monsignor, I treasure your friendship and hope to have it for the years ahead." But that was not to be, for three weeks later he suffered a heart attack and within a matter of a few days he was dead on June 10. Although our relationship had never been close it was invariably cordial, and I felt saddened by the loss of a churchman whom I had sincerely esteemed and admired.

I trust it is pardonable pride when a teacher finds it gratifying that his or her former students have made their mark in life. I have experienced that gratification in the case of a number of students I taught as undergraduates, to say nothing of those I have had the pleasure of directing as graduate students. In the former category I think especially of two members of the class of 1939 at the university, Roland Murphy and John Zeender, the former an internationally known Old Testament scholar, the latter a distinguished authority on modern German history who after his Yale doctorate and some years at the University of Massachusetts, Amherst, returned to Washington in 1959 where he has since had an enviable record for superior teaching. The class of 1940 numbered among other notable students Ernest L. Unterkoefler who since 1964 has been Bishop of Charleston, South Carolina. The next class of 1941 brought two men who from their freshman year (1937) made an outstanding impression, namely, James Collins, whose reputation as an historian of philosophy has long since established an enduring place in scholarly circles, and that far beyond Saint Louis University where he has taught since 1945, and his classmate and close friend, Humberto S. Medeiros who died on September 17, 1983, three weeks short of his sixty-eight birthday. Holding to the rule I made of treating only dead bishops, I should like to enter here some recollections of Boston's third cardinal archbishop.

Humberto Medeiros entered the Catholic University of America as a freshman in September, 1937, the son of poor immigrants from the Azores Islands. During his youth in Fall River he worked for a time sweeping floors in a factory for a mere pittance. He brought with him to Washington characteristics that marked him to the end of his life: deep faith, seriousness of purpose, unflagging industry, and a concern for others that was conspicuous. I have more than once remarked that Humberto and Jim used to write undergraduate term papers that would put to shame some master's theses that I read in later years. It was a new experience for me to have undergraduates who would quote from sources in foreign languages, something that Humberto and Jim would do with ease, and I was pleased when they enrolled in another of my courses during their sophomore year.

At the end of his sophomore year Humberto Medeiros entered upon his studies for the priesthood and was ordained for the Diocese of Fall River in 1946. I saw little of him thereafter, but was delighted to hear in 1966 that he had been named Bishop of Brownsville, Texas, where he made an outstanding record. I recall being told by my friend, Sister Mary Keating of the College of Saint Teresa, who spent a year or more on the missions in Brownsville that she was present on the day Medeiros departed for Boston in 1970, and she added, "We were all in tears." His talent for languages stood him in good stead among the large Hispanic population of the Texas diocese, and while he was said to be popular with most of his flock he was especially beloved among the Mexican working class whose rights and interests he championed more than once in their struggle for a living wage and decent working conditions. And he did so on his own terms, for he not only fought for justice for the workers but did not hesitate to challenge what he regarded as undue interference in his diocesan affairs from his metropolitan, Robert E. Lucey, Archbishop of San Antonio. In a word, the Brownsville appointment seemed a striking example of the right man in the right place.

The promotion of Humberto Medeiros as Archbishop of Boston was, to be sure, a promotion, but as time went on I gathered the impression that the move did not add to the archbishop's happiness. His Portuguese background ill fitted him for the heavily Irish enclave of Boston wherein he did not feel at home, so to speak. At times this must have brought real pain as, for example, when in March, 1973, he was in Rome to receive his new rank as a cardinal. A Boston priest told me that the new cardinal found himself with so many engagements on that occasion that he asked one of the Boston auxiliary bishops of Irish extraction to take his place at a Mass scheduled for those who had come to Rome for the ceremony. The congregation was predominantly of Portuguese background from Medeiro's family and friends of Fall River to whom the auxiliary preached a sermon on the glories of Ireland!

At the time of Medeiro's move to Boston in 1970 I received a telephone call in San Francisco from a Boston newspaper reporter who stated that they were finding it difficult to get the new archbishop to talk about himself and his background. The reporter said, "He has told us that you were his professor and to ask you about him." I gladly furnished information on his superior performance as a student and filled in as best I could about other features of his career. As the stormy 1970's continued Archbishop

Medeiros encountered a number of unpleasant episodes in his defense of the Church's teaching on abortion and other controversial issues such as social justice in neighborhoods like South Boston. In the midst of these public encounters when the media were almost always against him for his conservative stance, little heed was paid to the archbishop's dedicated service to his pastoral duties and his signal accomplishment in quietly paying off the enormous archdiocesan debt—variously estimated as high as $60,000,000— an achievement of no ordinary kind during a period of severe economic recession and widespread unemployment. I recall his telling me at dinner in Rome in the spring of 1975 that the debt then stood at $18,000,000, a notable figure when one recalls what he had inherited at Boston four years before.

While I cannot claim that I was a close friend of Cardinal Medeiros, we were on sufficiently cordial terms that I felt no hesitation when in Boston in calling on him where I was his guest several times for lunch or dinner. Our last meeting took place in March, 1978, when I went to Boston to visit my friend, Father Raymond G. Decker, who was spending a semester as an intern at the Harvard Law School. Ray was generous enough to give a dinner in my honor at the Hotel Commander in Cambridge to which the cardinal came along with a number of other friends like Martin Connor, James Hennesey, S.J., and Joseph Moody of the Boston College and Saint John's Seminary faculties. It was an altogether pleasant evening and Cardinal Medeiros invited Ray and me to dinner at his residence the following evening. He had recently been in Brazil where his misgivings were aroused about certain features of the liberation theology movement. As I recall it that was the principal subject of conversation and the cardinal was less than happy with the attempted defense offered by Ray and myself of that controversial movement in Latin America. It was my final meeting with my student of 40 years before, a churchman for whom I retained a genuine esteem even when I could not always agree with his opinions or the manner in which he chose to express them.

Apostolic Delegates

Although this work is primarily a memoir about American bishops, several persons whom I consulted thought I should include some comment on the apostolic delegates who served in Washington in my time. My first glimpse of a delegate occurred in the late 1920's when Archbishop Pietro Fumasoni-Biondi, a big lumbering sort of man, would come to the university or National Shrine for various functions. In those years I hardly knew what an apostolic delegate was, let alone have a personal acquaintance with one. It was only with the arrival of Fumasoni-Biondi's successor, Amleto G. Cicognani, in 1933 that I became acquainted with the pope's representative in the United States, and my first encounter was not a very happy one. The delegate came to the seminary one morning to offer Mass and I was appointed to serve him. While putting on the maniple I stuck his arm with the pin at which he let forth a muffled cry of pain. It was scarcely an auspicious beginning!

After my ordination to the priesthood in 1938 I would meet Archbishop Cicognani from time to time at ecclesiastical functions, especially when he was the presiding prelate and I was the preacher, for example, at the inauguration in

1944 of the Academy of American Franciscan History which was held at the Franciscan Monastery near the university. Another occasion was the year I was asked to preach the sermon for the anniversary of Pius XII's coronation on March 12 when an unnamed bishop found it impossible to fulfill the assignment and I was requested to substitute for him. My only memory of that first luncheon at the Apostolic Delegation was my absorption in conversation that left me the only one at table still eating until Cicognani looked my way, asked if I was finished, and hurried my pace with some embarrassment. But the reminder was very gently given, as was always true of this tactful and polite prelate, whose courtesy I especially appreciated when in the spring of 1946 my mother visited Washington and at the instance of my friend, Monsignor Cartwright, the delegate received us and was warm and attentive to all of us, especially to my mother.

Several years later another meeting went beyond a brief social call at the Delegation. At the end of World War II the archives of the German foreign office, hidden in the Harz Mountains by the Nazis when their fortunes were in swift decline, were discovered by the allied armies. The governments of France, Great Britain, and the United States each appointed a group of historians to edit the documents with the result that they were published in multi-volume series by the respective governments. The chief American editor was Raymond J. Sontag, Ehrman professor of modern history in the University of California, Berkeley, a personal friend of mine and a devout Catholic. One volume of this series that came out in 1949 included a lengthy chapter entitled, "German Relations with the Holy See, March 1937-September 1938." Since there were no diplomatic relations between the Holy See and the United States the delegate, unlike the ambassadors of countries with such official relations, was not entitled to be shown copies of the documents.

Good Catholic as he was, Ray Sontag was concerned that

the delegate not be taken by surprise by this publication. One afternoon I received a telephone call from Monsignor Joseph McShea, the delegate's secretary, asking if I would do a piece of work for Cicognani. I said I would be glad to do so and inquired what it was, only to be told that he could not mention the subject over the telephone. Would I be in for an hour or so? Yes, I expected to be at home for the remainder of the afternoon. In that case Father Edward Stanford, O.S.A., of the Augustinian College would contact me. In about a half hour Stanford called, asked the same question to which I gave the same answer and inquired about the nature of the assignment, with the result I received the identical reply, it could not be mentioned over the telephone. Might he come to my apartment in Caldwell Hall? I stated yes, of course, all the while growing more and more curious to know what lay behind the mysterious telephone calls. Upon arrival Father Stanford explained the matter—he and Ray were close friends—and I consented to go to the Augustinian College several days later to read the chapter in question, make notes on the documents for my own information, and then, in turn, give the delegate an oral report on their contents.

Subsequently I spent the better part of a day reading the galleys of a chapter that was ultimately published in about 125 pages. When I finished I joined Ray and Edward Stanford and the former asked me to call the Delegation to make an appointment with Archbishop Cicognani, to report to him orally but to leave nothing in writing in his possession. In due course I went to Massachusetts Avenue where I proceeded to summarize the documents for Cicognani. I told him the Holy See need have no worry about their contents, that Pius XI and Cardinal Pacelli came through strongly in opposition to the Nazis. In only two instances, I said, was the action of the Catholic churchmen a source of embarrassment. "Who were they?" he asked, to which I replied Bishop Hudal, Rector of the German College at

Rome. "Oh, yes, everyone knew he was pro-Nazi," said Cicognani. And the other, I added, was Cardinal Theodore Innitzer, Archbishop of Vienna, who was found welcoming the Nazis to his see city. This name was likewise no surprise to the delegate, and he remarked, "You know his appointment was a mistake. He was a professor," and then realizing he was talking to a professor he sought to retrieve the slip by adding, "I mean some professors." I was highly amused at the ever-cautious delegate's lapse. When he asked if I would leave him my notes I informed him I was instructed to make only an oral report, whereupon he asked if he might take notes as I spoke, a suggestion to which I readily agreed. For me it was a pleasant duty to perform this minor task for all concerned, while at the same time increasing my own knowledge about the delicate and often stormy relations between the Vatican and the Berlin government of those hectic years.

Another occasion that brought Archbishop Cicognani and me together was the annual rally at the Monument Grounds in Washington for the feast of Christ the King. on Sunday, October 26, 1947. Again he was presiding and I was the preacher. Once President Franklin Roosevelt had appointed Myron Taylor as his personal representative at the Holy See in December, 1939, the question of diplomatic relations between this country and the Vatican continued to be a source of controversy, a controversy that erupted repeatedly until in the aftermath of vociferous opposition to the appointment in 1951 of General Mark Clark as ambassador prompted the general some time later to ask President Truman to withdraw his nomination. In the course of my sermon on that Sunday afternoon in 1947 I devoted a portion to this highly sensitive issue. Speaking of Myron Taylor's presence at the Vatican, I stated:

> Whether or not Mr. Taylor remains at Vatican City is the concern and business of the President of the United States and

Archbishop Cicognani

the Department of State... American Catholics—as Catholics—are entirely indifferent whether he remains or returns, for they know the quality of their religious faith does not rise or fall on the shaky scaffolding of diplomatic representation of their Government at Vatican City.[18]

I added that as Americans the Catholics of this country might well regret the loss to their government of the information to be had at the Holy See if the president felt "compelled to yield before the specious reasoning of a noisy few who profess to see a peril to the American doctrine of separation of Church and State in Mr. Taylor's mission."[19]

At the end of the ceremony I accompanied Archbishop Cicognani and Father Joseph Moran, archdiocesan Director of the Holy Name Society that had sponsored the rally,

[18]Washington *Post*, October 27, 1947, p. 2B.

[19]*Catholic Review* (Baltimore), October 31, 1947, p. 14. The full text of the sermon was carried here, a copy of which I owe to the kindness of Sister Felicitas Powers, R.S.M., archivist of the Archdiocese of Baltimore.

back to the Delegation. On the way nothing was said about the sermon, and when we arrived at 3339 Massachusetts Avenue we got out to bid the delegate farewell when he turned to me and said, "You said many things." "Yes," I replied, "perhaps too many things." That was all and we parted, as I later remarked, with a Mona Lisa smile that left our true sentiments unexpressed. The following day the Washington *Post* carried a story on the event with several quotations from the sermon. Going into lunch I met Jerome D. Hannan, professor of canon law, who made no secret of wishing to be bishop. He asked, "Did you say what today's *Post* quotes you as saying?" I replied that I had, which prompted another question, "Was the delegate present?" Yes, the delegate was present, and then Hannan quietly stated, "Maybe that is the way to become a bishop." The same canon lawyer achieved his ambition in 1954 when he was named Bishop of Scranton without expressing publicly what he thought about diplomatic relations between the United States and the Holy See.

Before nightfall the rumor was abroad on the campus that I had been rebuked by Cicognani. Nothing of the kind had occurred, although I was reasonably certain that he found some of my remarks other than to his liking. Whatever may have been his true reaction to the sermon, he showed no outward sign of disapproval, and at the Saint Patrick's Day luncheon in 1953 in the course of his customary speech about the island of saints and scholars, he suddenly turned in my direction and stated, "I see Father Ellis at the end of the table. I want to congratulate him on his life of Cardinal Gibbons. Oh, there are a few pages about which I would have some doubts, but all in all it is a great work." The candor of the Gibbons biography had caused some uneasiness to my ordinary, Archbishop Patrick O'Boyle, who that day standing at the door to bid good-by to his guests said to me with evident relief, "Now you have finally been approved." I was gratified that my efforts to write the

Church's history as it had actually happened, 'warts and all,' to quote the familiar expression, had ultimately won their acceptance.

Archbishop Cicognani's tenure of the Apostolic Delegation was about four times longer than any of his predecessors or successors. He arrived in the United States in the spring of 1933 and did not depart until December, 1958, when Pope John XXIII made him a cardinal in his first consistory. The reason for the lengthy stay, it was commonly believed, was that he had incurred the displeasure of Pius XII by his disapproval of the latter's visit to this country in 1936. It was also said that he was against Pacelli's being a guest of the papal duchess, Genevieve Garvan Brady MacCauley, at Inisfada, her Long Island estate. Cardinal Hayes told my friend, Monsignor Charles E. Fitzgerald, that he too was opposed to the Secretary of State stopping there, but there was nothing he could do about it. These opinions of Cicognani were said to have reached the pontiff and he did not forget them and hence kept the delegate at a distance.

Whatever the motive, the fact was all too evident. I used to remark that the delegate was in the 'papal doghouse,' but it was a very comfortable one. An English priest, Father John Redmond, had helped Cicognani to learn English at Rome, and when Redmond came one summer on a holiday to the United States he visited Cicognani who received him warmly. Redmond later told us at the university where he was stopping that he asked, "Why are you not a cardinal?" to which Cicognani realistically replied, "I will not be a cardinal in this pontificate." His situation was immediately changed, however, with the coming of Pope John XXIII. In the ceremony immediately following the conclave when the cardinals made their individual obeisance to the newly elected pope, John XXIII leaned over to the delegate's brother, Cardinal Gaetano Cicognani, and said, "I will not forget your brother," or words to that effect. In the sequel not only did the pope carry out his promise by making Amleto Cicognani a cardinal, but at the death of Domenico Tardini in 1961 he named him Secretary of State, a post he held as well during the early years of Paul VI.

While he resided in the United States I was never aware that Cicognani was other than *persona grata* to the great majority of American bishops and clergy. He was extraordinarily discreet and held himself aloof from matters that did not fall within his jurisdiction. In fact, it would have been difficult to identify the delegate's ideology other than the fact that he followed traditional views and policies. Upon his return to Rome, however, he showed a rather marked conservative turn of mind, and during Vatican Council II he was frequently aligned with the party of the right. For example, when the latter sought to block a vote on religious freedom in September, 1965, Cicognani was one of the four key figures summoned by Paul VI on the morning of September 21 to be told there would be a vote on religious freedom. As I watched him cross the floor of Saint Peter's after the Mass had begun that morning I did not realize the reason for his being late for the session. If this conservative stance was a disappointment to some of Cicognani's American admirers, all in all he retained their high regard and good will. Near the end of his time as Secretary of State when he had reached his late eighties and was thought by many too old to continue, he held on to the office until Paul VI was practically forced to replace him with a younger man, much to the old man's chagrin. I remember Monsignor Richard Mahowald, superior of the Casa Santa Maria in my time there, telling me that when he visited Cicognani on his ninetieth birthday the cardinal remarked to my friend, "That pope was here yesterday and brought me a bottle of champagne." It was evident that he had not been won over by the pontiff's gesture.

If Archbishop Cicognani earned high marks for his tact and discretion during his long residence in the United

Archbishop Vagnozzi

States, his successor, Archbishop Egidio Vagnozzi, was less distinguished in that regard. He arrived in May, 1959, and two months later I had my first conversation with him. The occasion was the sesquicentennial of the founding by Saint Elizabeth Seton of her religious community at Emmitsburg, Maryland. The delegate was the celebrant of the Mass and I had been asked to preach. The evening before we were the guests of the Daughters of Charity at dinner, that is, a group of about a dozen clergymen with Bishop John McNamara on the delegate's right and I on his left. Suddenly Vagnozzi remarked, "The President is anti-Catholic." There was a moment of stunned silence, and then I made bold to say, "Excuse me, archbishop, that is not true. He appointed Robert Murphy as Undersecretary of State, Jefferson Caffrey as Ambassador to Egypt..." Fortunately, several names of Catholics came quickly to mind who had been appointed to high posts by President Eisenhower. "Oh, is that so," said Vagnozzi and changed the subject. While we were all conscious of various faults of Dwight Eisenhower, I doubt it would have entered any American's head to accuse him of anti-Catholicism. All things considered, it was a rather disconcerting experience.

The incident at the Emmitsburg dinner was, needless to say, a private one and known only to the few who were present. More serious was Vagnozzi's baccalaureate sermon at Marquette University in June, 1961. It came at a time of considerable tension within the Catholic community over the real or alleged abuses of academic freedom. In August, 1950, Pius XII's encyclical, *Humani generis*, had sounded a note of warning about the need for vigilance in holding to orthodox teaching, and in the ensuing decade a number of prominent intellectuals such as John Courtney Murray, S.J., Yves Congar, O.P., *et al.*, had come under a cloud at Rome. At Milwaukee the delegate noted the threat to the Church from "the modern massive opposition of secularism and naturalism," but his most pointed remarks were directed to certain unnamed Catholic intellectuals about whom he said *inter alia*:

> The complaint has been voiced more than once that in high ecclesiastical circles the intellectual is often underestimated and also mistrusted. The question is whether we are confronted with true and genuine intellectuals, who are inspired by a sincere love of truth, humbly disposed to submit to God's Revelation and the authority of His Church, or whether we are confronted with intellectuals who believe, first of all, in the absolute supremacy and unlimited freedom of human reason, a reason which has shown itself so often fallacious and subject to error.[20]

The sermon caused something of a sensation and became the subject of open criticism among American Catholics in academia.

Archbishop Vagnozzi was a genial person at social gath-

---

[20]John Tracy Ellis, "A Tradition of Autonomy?", Neil G. McCluskey (Ed.), *The Catholic University. A Modern Appraisal.* Notre Dame: University of Notre Dame Press. 1970. p. 265.

erings where his sprightly remarks and fine singing voice
added to the joy and entertainment. But these agreeable
qualities did not weigh heavily enough to balance the fairly
frequent public expressions on delicate questions that did
not come within the scope of his official duties. After I had
come to know Archbishop Igino Cardinale, then Apostolic
Delegate to Great Britain and after 1969 Nuncio to Belgium,
I felt free to ask this very approachable and open churchman how he was to account for Vagnozzi's appointment to
Washington. As one who had served as Pope John XXIII's
chief of protocol he had close knowledge of such matters.

Archbishop Cardinale told me that in the time that Vagnozzi served as auditor of the Paris nunciature when the
then Archbishop Angelo Roncalli was nuncio, the auditor
would be heard to say to the nuncio on occasion, "You don't
know what you are talking about." Yet it was the same
Roncalli who as John XXIII appointed Vagnozzi, then
Nuncio to the Philippines, to the Delegation in Washington.
When I confessed that I found it difficult to understand,
Cardinale remarked, "It was Pope John's policy to be kind
to his enemies." We agreed that such a policy was admirable
on the spiritual plane, but that it could prove damaging on
the mundane level of human affairs. Be that as it may, at the
end of his time as delegate Egidio Vagnozzi was in 1967
named a cardinal with assignment to the Roman Curia. I
have more than once pondered that phenomenon, namely,
the promotion to the College of Cardinals of prelates whose
careers had been less than a success—Carlo Chiarlo, the
Nuncio to Brazil, whom I have mentioned previously comes
to mind. It is only one more of the minor mysteries of life
about which I expect to die as uninformed as I have lived.

The 'mystery' surrounding the advancement of some
churchmen to the cardinalate is, however, often only figura-
tively so. If the Church is divine, which I firmly believe, she
is also on occasion all too human in revealing the sins, the
faulty judgments, and the blunders of certain of her princi-

pal officers. Lacordaire, the famous French Dominican, once put the point in a memorable way when he told a professor of church history in the Sorbonne:

> God indeed has conferred upon His Church the prerogative of infallibility, but to none of her members has He granted immunity from sin. Peter was a sinner and a renegade, and God has been at pains to have the fact recorded in the Gospels.[21]

The history of the College of Cardinals has recorded the same. If Pope Alexander VI's making his illegitimate son, Cesare Borgia, a cardinal in 1493 at the age of 18 was perhaps the most notorious of these nominations, there have been numerous other cases of unworthy candidates through the centuries.

The past century has seen a distinct improvement in that regard, and the naming of profligate characters such as Borgia has long since ceased. Moreover, the practice of automatically making cardinals of ordinaries of certain dioceses and nuncios to particular countries, not to mention long-serving officials of the Roman Curia, would likewise seem to be on the wane. The nomination of 18 new cardinals by Pope John Paul II in February, 1983, reflected that change with traditional cardinalitial sees like Munich and Seville passed over as well as nuncios and curial officials who in former days would have been among the nominees. It is a healthy sign that augurs well for the further internationalization of the College of Cardinals with new members from unexpected places like Bangkok and Riga. Yet the human element remains and the sophisticated observer will be aware that at some future date cronyism may reappear, to say nothing of the success of aggressively ambitious clerics, while much more worthy churchmen remain unrewarded. As I once heard it said in another context, this is the

[21]Lacordaire to Henri Perreyve, April 2, 1855, Joseph T. Foisset, *Vie du R. Père Lacordaire*. Paris: Lecoffre fils et Cie. 1870. II, 532.

price the Church must pay for being in the human condition.

Of the apostolic delegates who followed Egidio Vagnozzi, less need be said. The last two to serve in that office, Archbishops Jean Jadot and Pio Laghi, are happily still living and, therefore, do not come within the compass of this memoir. Parenthetically, I may say that of all the delegates to the United States I have had friendlier relations with these two than any others. As for Vagnozzi's immediate successor, Archbishop Luigi Raimondi, I personally know of little to be said. Perhaps that is due to my lack of contact or close acquaintance with the delegate during the years from 1967 to 1973. It may likewise be accounted for by his extraordinary reticence, for he was so quiet that it suggested the thought that he may have been chosen deliberately as one who would help to eliminate the ruffled feelings left in some quarters by his outspoken predecessor. As far as I can now recall I heard Archbishop Raimondi speak in public only once, namely, at the 1970 spring meeting of the hierarchy in Detroit. His brief address to the bishops was so discreet that had a newspaper man been present he would, I think, have been at a loss to know what to report of it. At his entrance the bishops stood and applauded in a manner becoming to the pope's representative; there seemed less reason for the same action when the delegate took his departure from the conference room. Luigi Raimondi was made a cardinal in 1973 and appointed Prefect of the Congregation for the Causes of Saints, a post he had held for a short time when he died of a heart attack in June, 1975.

It is now nearly a century since Pope Leo XIII established the Apostolic Delegation in Washington in 1893. I devoted a lengthy chapter to its origins and early history in the biography of Cardinal Gibbons. Of the 14 archbishops of that time only one, John Ireland of Saint Paul, was in favor of the Delegation. In fact, they took energetic steps to prevent its realization, but they failed. Were they mistaken in their action? Had I been living in the 1890's I suspect I would have been on the side of the opposition for many of the same reasons advanced by the archbishops, for example, that it would arouse anti-Catholic sentiment, that it would lessen the authority of the bishops in their individual dioceses, etc.

The history of the Delegation in this country, however, has taught me—as, I believe, it has the great majority of American Catholics—that the fears of the 1890's were largely unfounded. True, there have been moments of tension when an apostolic delegate's words or actions have prompted American resentment, but what human situation involving conflicting ideas has been free of periodic tension of this kind? When the Delegation's record of 90 years is weighed in the balance, however, historians will, I think, conclude that its positive contribution to the welfare of the American Church has outweighed the negative aspects of its activities. Not only has this been true of the institution's role as an arbiter of disputes among Catholics of the United States, but as well of the vital part it plays in the selection of bishops. To be sure, here and there the judgment of apostolic delegates in the choice of bishops has been proven faulty, but again when measured against the over-all results and the inherent weaknesses attendant upon other methods of selection, the record would, I am convinced, sustain the present system, allowing always for the broader consultation on these choices outlined in Paul VI's *motu proprio* "Concerning the Office of Representatives of the Pope," of June 24, 1969.

When Christopher Sykes paid a visit to Evelyn Waugh at a time when the latter was writing his autobiography he told him he had become fearful now that Waugh was getting into Volume II which, said Sykes, "will spill over into me."[22] As I

[22]Christopher Sykes, *Evelyn Waugh. A Biography*. Boston: Little, Brown and Company. 1975. p. 445. Sykes and his wife had just come from T.S. Eliot's funeral, little knowing that Waugh would himself die suddenly the following day from a heart attack. (Easter Sunday, April 18, 1965). His description of Waugh's state of mind on that final visit makes rather sad reading. Syke wrote:

draw toward the close of these memoirs I have to renew my original purpose that they will treat solely bishops who have gone to their reward, lest I should be tempted to 'spill over' into living prelates, about some of whom I have the fondest recollections, while of others my views and impressions are more negative than I should wish. That approach is at least in conformity with a generally accepted principle of historians that attempting contemporary history is to enter upon a slippery terrain. In that regard Denis Mack Smith put it well when he declared:

> Anyone who tries to write on contemporary affairs...will know the impossibility of being perfectly judicial and accurate in a field where tempers have not yet cooled and the pattern of history has not had time to set.[23]

While I have made a conscientious effort to be 'judicial and accurate,' I am under no illusion that I have struck a perfect balance. For to do otherwise is to take oneself with a seriousness that carries one out of the real world and into a world of fantasy such as that inhabited by Claude Robin, an eccentric priest of the Diocese of Angers, of whom it was said:

> He believed his writings were destined to immortality, and to make assurance doubly sure, he immured copies of his books in walls and public monuments for the benefit of future archaeologists.[24]

He sighed and with a sudden change from the joking manner of our conversation he said: 'You've no reason to fear. No one has. I wish they had. My life is roughly speaking over. I sleep badly except occasionally in the morning. I get up late. I try to read my letters. I try to read the paper. I have some gin. I try to read the paper again. I have some more gin. I try to think about my autobiography, then I have some more gin and it's lunch time. That's my life. It's ghastly.

[23]Denis Mack Smith, *Italy. A Modern History.* New edition, revised and enlarged. Ann Arbor: University of Michigan Press. 1969. p. vi.

[24]John McManners, *French Ecclesiastical Society under the Ancien Regime. A Study of Angers in the Eighteenth Century.* Manchester: Manchester University Press. 1960. p. 183.

In the Service of Clio

By reason of speaking engagements in various dioceses, research trips for the biography of Cardinal Gibbons and other historical works, and residence at the university, I came to have a passing acquaintance with a good number of other bishops. In that category there come to mind two archbishops who made clear to me that they had a concern in common, namely, the retrieval of documents from their archdiocesan archives that had years before been given over by their predecessors to James F. Edwards (d. 1911), a lay historian at the University of Notre Dame who had traveled around the country gathering papers for what he called the Catholic Archives of America.

While doing research in Cincinnati I called on John T. McNicholas, O.P., the archbishop, who expressed his chagrin at the loss of the Cincinnati papers to Notre Dame and said he felt they should be returned. 'Did I think that Notre Dame would give them back'? Knowing the vigilance that Father Tom McAvoy exercised over Notre Dame's collections, I told him I thought there was little likelihood of a return of the originals, but perhaps he might have copies made. I was left with the impression that McNicholas did not consider that a satisfactory solution to the problem, but in the sequel the Cincinnati documents remained at Notre Dame.

The second case was that of Joseph F. Rummel, Archbishop of New Orleans. I was in New Orleans in May, 1960, for the commencement address at Saint Mary's Dominican College and the archbishop invited me to lunch. By this time the eighty-three year old prelate was almost blind and had mellowed a good deal. He brought up the subject of the New Orleans documents and like his counterpart in Cincinnati, asked if I thought Notre Dame would return them. I gave the same answer as I had to McNicholas some years before, but in this instance Rummel seemed content and remarked with a reconciled air, "They are probably better cared for there than they would be here." It was a sound judgment, for historians of American Catholicism were well aware of the careful preservation that Tom McAvoy gave to the papers in his custody.

During the years that the Gibbons biography was in preparation I traveled all over the nation in search of archival material. In most dioceses I was given *carte blanche* and treated with genuine courtesy and generosity by the local diocesan officials, but there were several exceptions. I met my first complete roadblock in Tucson where Bishop Daniel J. Gercke was personally friendly enough but quite adamant against admitting me to the archives, tossing off the subject in a rather light-hearted way by saying, "You wouldn't be interested in anything we have here." Needless to say, I would have preferred to determine that for myself, but there was no opportunity to do so. Had the local ordinary in Savannah, Gerald P. O'Hara, been at home in January, 1948, when I went there from New Orleans, I think I might have fared differently. The vicar general would not hear of my seeing the archives. It happened that the Bishop of Charleston, Emmet M. Walsh, a charming man, was at the Savannah cathedral that morning for a wedding. I appealed to him and he, in turn, made a plea in my behalf but the vicar general remained unmoved. Incidentally, I rode with Bishop Walsh to Charleston later in the day and was his guest for overnight at the cathedral rectory. He was one of the best story-tellers I have ever met and on the ride to Charleston, through dinner and the early evening he regaled me with one story after another, interrupted at one point, as I remember, by the startling news that Gandhi had been assassinated that day.

I should like to comment here about several bishops whose training or experience would classify them as historians. While throughout the nineteenth and early twentieth centuries there were numerous teachers of history in Catholic seminaries and colleges, the professionally trained man in those posts was virtually non-existent. For example, the first professor of church history, properly so-called, in the Catholic University of America, Thomas O'Gorman, a priest of the Archdiocese of Saint Paul who had taught for some years in the archdiocesan seminary, had no formal training in history when he assumed his duties at Washington in September, 1890. O'Gorman taught church history for five years and was then named Bishop of Sioux Falls where he remained until his death in 1921. Of his success or failure as an historian, I have never seen any evidence, so I cannot say whether or not O'Gorman was one of those that Archbishop John Ireland had in mind when he counseled the university rector, "You must educate your professors, & then hold on to them—making bishops only of those who are not worth keeping as professors."[25]

When I think of the low estate of history in Catholic institutions in those years I am reminded of a story told me by my friend and colleague, Father Francis P. Cassidy, an

[25]John Ireland to John J. Keane, Rome, April 26, 1892, Patrick Henry Ahern, *The Catholic University of America, 1887-1896. The Rectorship of John J. Keane.* Washington: The Catholic University of America Press. 1948. p. 50.

alumnus of Mount Saint Mary's College in Emmitsburg.
Frank said that when Pascal Robinson, O.F.M., who taught
medieval history at the university in Washington (1913-
1919), made his first visit to Emmitsburg he inquired of the
president, Monsignor Bernard Bradley, who taught history
there. Bradley turned to his long-time associate, John J.
Tierney, and asked, "Who's teaching history this year?" If
the learned friar, who died in 1948 after nearly twenty years
as Nuncio to Ireland, was mildly surprised at the reply, it
revealed where history then ranked, and that in more
schools than Mount Saint Mary's.

By the 1920's matters had begun to improve a bit in that
regard and future bishops such as Thomas K. Gorman and
James L. Connolly took their doctorates in ecclesiastical
history at the Catholic University of Louvain. Gorman
doubtless found his historical training of use as editor of
The Tidings, the weekly newspaper of his native Diocese of
Los Angeles. But he had little opportunity beyond that since
in 1931 he was named first Bishop of Reno and in 1952 was
transferred to the Diocese of Dallas. I became acquainted
with Bishop Gorman while I was living with Fulton Sheen,
his Louvain schoolmate, with whom he stopped when he
came to Washington for the meetings of the hierarchy. We
used to take walks after dinner through Wesley Heights and
Spring Valley when he entertained me with accounts of his
frontier diocese, for example, how he would go to Chicago
for the annual meeting of the Catholic Church Extension
Society and there make eloquent appeals for funds from the
Society's chancellor, Cardinal Mundelein, by dwelling on
the crop failures and any other local calamity that came to
mind. Gorman related to me how the Diocese of Reno came
to be erected. He said that Mundelein was passing through
Nevada on one occasion on a train from California and
inquired who was the bishop there. When informed that
there was no bishop in Nevada, the cardinal maintained that
the dignity of the Church demanded that there should be a

diocese in every state and he would see to the matter and, if necessary, support the venture. When the first bishop was selected from Los Angeles and not by the Cardinal of Chicago, so Gorman remarked, Mundelein's enthusiasm for the Church of Nevada cooled quite a degree.

It so happened that Reno's second bishop, Robert J. Dwyer, was also trained as an historian, having taken his doctorate at the Catholic University of America in 1941 with a lengthy and able dissertation published under the title, *The Gentile Comes to Utah.* Dwyer was a native of Salt Lake City and hence knew the local scene at first hand. With the exception of Archbishop Paul Hallinan, about whom I will treat in due course, Robert Dwyer probably employed his historical knowledge more than any bishop schooled in that discipline. For the most part his writings consisted of newspaper articles which he contributed regularly to the Catholic press, a practice he continued through his years as Archbishop of Portland in Oregon (1966-1974). Those devoted to historical themes revealed a detailed knowledge of the Church's history and were, I think, widely appreciated.

By reason of our interest in history and, too, of our mutual friendship with another historian, John B. McGloin, S.J., of the University of San Francisco, I came to know Bishop Dwyer quite well. More than once he asked me to visit him in Reno, which I did late one summer during my last years of residence in California. From time to time I had received appeals from the 'Desert Bishop of Reno,' if I recall accurately the identification on his stationery, and I responded on occasion with a mite for the Nevada missions.

When I arrived in Reno on that hot summer day I was met at the airport by the bishop in his air-conditioned Cadillac wherein the white pekingese occupied a spot near its master, and the next morning at breakfast the pekingese was even more favored by resting in the master's lap. I seem to recall that Dwyer came from a family of means and was accustomed to the good life, which was manifest in his attractive residence where everything was in the best of taste. If I was momentarily taken back by the surroundings of the 'desert bishop,' I was even more impressed, I believe, by the size and solid content of the bishop's library. With the exception of the library of the late Douglas Woodruff, longtime editor of *The Tablet* of London, I doubt that I have ever seen a private library as large and containing a finer collection of books in history, literature, and the ecclesiastical sciences. Here, indeed, was evidence that the ordinary of a missionary diocese had maintained his intellectual interests.

I have had occasion to mention several bishops who in their later life showed a marked conservative turn of mind, for example, Sheen, Cicognani, and Wright. This was equally true of Robert Dwyer. In the period after Vatican Council II his writings demonstrated more and more distress at developments within the Church. Both Wright and Dwyer were keen students of Cardinal Newman; yet Newman's oft-quoted axiom, "In a higher world it is otherwise, but here below to live is to change, and to be perfect is to have changed often," seemed to have had little influence on their thinking in the post-conciliar age. It was a pity, for these men had richly stored minds that could have given direction and guidance during that 'uncertain, anxious time.'

Unfortunately, Bishop Dwyer and others were so completely alienated by what they regarded as policies and opinions that posed a threat to the Church's doctrine and tradition—and there were, to be sure, reasons for anxiety on that score in the case of some Catholics—that at times a note suggesting bitterness entered their public pronouncements. Given their knowledge of church history one might have thought it would have served as an assurance that extreme positions would in time pass and that certain innovations would prove to have been salutary for the Catholic community.

In any case, I became aware that Dwyer had come to reckon me as in the camp of the enemy, a fact made evident from the coolness with which he greeted me at our last chance meeting in a hotel lobby in Washington one evening. I likewise learned this from his remark in one of his newspaper columns that Ellis' "vitriolic pen" was in motion again. At the moment I cannot remember what I had said that offended this once friendly prelate. The experience was not unique, for in March, 1973, when I spoke at the luncheon honoring my lifelong friend, John L. McMahon, as President of Our Lady of the Lake College in San Antonio, both the retired archbishop, Robert E. Lucey, and the ordinary of that time, Francis J. Furey, absented themselves from the luncheon due to a recent remark of mine about the plausibility of the retirement of Pope Paul VI in view of the latter's ruling that bishops should retire at age seventy-five. In this instance I felt sincere regret for my off-hand remark because of my affection and esteem for John McMahon and, too, my increasing regard for Paul VI's contribution to the Church's welfare in an uncommonly difficult span of years.

Archbishop Cardinale

Now and then there comes news of the death of a bishop that carries a touch of personal sadness. I experienced that in March, 1983, in learning of the death of Archbishop Igino Cardinale, Apostolic Nuncio to Belgium, Luxembourg, and the European Economic Community. I first met this gracious and friendly churchman at Rome in the summer of 1965 when I attended the first Mass and reception of an American priest, the nephew of a friend of mine, at which Cardinale preached the homily in the chapel of the Capranica College. At the time he was Apostolic Delegate to Great Britain and when he learned I was going to London he invited me to visit him. Over a pleasant luncheon at the delegation in Wimbledon he told me and my friend, Ray Decker of San Francisco, a number of revealing stories about Pope John XXIII whom he had served as chief of protocol. I have already mentioned Cardinale's account of how Vagnozzi came to be named Apostolic Delegate to the United States in 1959.

More significant was Igino Cardinale's story concerning the chagrin felt by Pope Pius XII for General Charles de Gaulle who as head of the French government following the

fall of the Nazis had refused to receive Archbishop Valerio
Valeri, the nuncio, because the latter had in 1940 gone to
Vichy with the government of Marshal Henri Philippe
Pétain. Pius XII finally recalled Valeri and left the Paris
nunciature vacant for a time. Then, according to Cardinale,
to show his disdain for de Gaulle the pope reached down to
the lower ranks of the diplomatic ladder and sent Angelo
Roncalli from Istanbul to Paris. I confess that the explana-
tion was an eyeopener for me on several counts: first, that
Roncalli was held in such low esteem by Pius XII and,
secondly, that there was such ill feeling on his part for de
Gaulle.

Saint Ambrose once remarked, "It is normal that anyone
who wishes to be believed should establish his credibility."[26]
Cardinale had no difficulty in doing just that, and everything I later heard or read of matters on which he spoke was
borne out by others. The archbishop had been born in Italy
in 1916, but he spent his boyhood in Boston to which his
parents had immigrated for some years before returning to
their homeland where the future nuncio was ordained in
1941. His American residence would probably explain his
flawless English, although he was fluent in other languages
as well. He kept a warm spot in his heart for the United
States, and it was an open secret that he would have been
delighted to have been named apostolic delegate to this
country. The appointment never came, but I was reliably
informed that upon the departure of Archbishop Jadot in
1980 he was, along with the nuncios to Argentina and
Brazil, among the three leading candidates for the post.

After our initial meeting we corresponded from time to
time, and when I was in Brussels in the summer of 1969—
again with Ray Decker—he invited us to dinner where
Father Francis Sweeney, S.J., of Boston College was also a

---

[26]Gabriel Tissot, O.S.B. (Trans. and Ed.), *Ambroise de Milan. Traité sure
l'Evangile de S. Luc.* Paris: Darton, Longman & Todd. 1962. p. 133.

guest. The nuncio had recently returned from Rome where, he said, in an audience of Paul VI he had suggested that he be allowed to handle in his own way the delicate relations with Cardinal Leo Suenens, Primate of Belgium. Precisely what the problem was, he did not say. He made no secret of his hurt feelings, however, in being told after his audience that the pope had remarked he might burn his fingers. "This," he exclaimed with a show of deep emotion, "after twenty years of devoted service to the Holy See."

I recall that during dinner the nuncio and I had a somewhat heated discussion about *The Tablet* of London. He contended that it was doing harm to the Church by its sharp criticism of ecclesiastical affairs, and I maintained that I thought it was fundamentally loyal and that it was rendering a service by its critical approach. It spoke well for Cardinale's spirit of openness that he permitted this sort of difference of opinion at his own table. Not only did he accompany us to the automobile upon our departure and suggest that

Monsignor John Tracy Ellis, Archbishop Igino E. Cardinale, and the Reverend William J. Greytak, Rector of the American college at Leuven.

we return the next time we were in Brussels, but in our subsequent correspondence he showed not the slightest evidence of pique.

Thirteen years elapsed before I saw Archbishop Cardinale again. In the interval we exchanged letters a few times, the last relating to the book of Roland Flamini, *Pope, Premier, President. The Cold War Summit That Never Was* (1980), a volume dealing with the Cuban missile crisis in which Cardinale was mentioned a number of times. I informed him that I was scheduled to give two lectures in commemoration of the 125th anniversary of the American College at Leuven (Louvain) in early December, 1982, to which he quickly responded with a warm welcome. He drove out from Brussels for the Mass on December 8 at which the King and Queen of the Belgians were the honored guests, along with Cardinal Suenens, several other bishops, and the wives of Secretary of State George P. Shultz and the American Ambassador to Belgium, Charles Price. He came again for my evening lecture on December 9 after which he invited the Rector of the American College, William J. Greytak, and me for lunch at the nunciature in Brussels.

Archbishop Cardinale was anxious that I should see the new nunciature the construction of which he had overseen a few years before, a vast improvement over the rather somber old structure in which I had dined in 1969. Present at the luncheon was Canon Joseph Dessain, a specialist in ecumenism and a relative of my lamented friend, Stephen Dessain of the Oratory at Birmingham, England, the principal editor of the superb edition of the multi-volume *Letters and Diaries of John Henry Newman.* As was his custom, Cardinale presided with ease and grace, allowing the conversation to flow back and forth on any topic suggested by his guests. He had a good sense of humor and laughed frequently. It was understandable, therefore, that others should feel entirely comfortable in his presence, for he never tried to dominate a gathering and was altogether free of the stuffiness that overtakes some people in his position.

At that time he was anticipating the publication of his book on the history of knighthoods about which I listened politely, but it was a subject on which, I confess, I could not muster much enthusiasm. I had been more interested in his 1962 work on the Holy See and diplomacy and his book, *The Holy See and the International Order* (1976). I little thought as I bade Igino Cardinale farewell on that December afternoon that I had seen him for the last time. His death has been another recent reminder that the longer we live the more does the number of valued friends and associates thin out, but *c'est la vie* and one must make the best of it, grateful for the happy memories that they have left to us.

Facile Princeps
Archbishop Paul Hallinan

Before I treat of Paul Hallinan, one of the great bishops of my time, I wish to say something about one of his closest friends in the hierarchy, a bishop who was extraordinarily kind to me, Robert E. Tracy (1909-1980). And in placing my recollections of Bob Tracy at this particular point I am morally certain that our lamented friend of Atlanta would understand and approve. This New Orleans-born priest gained national attention in Catholic circles as chaplain of Louisiana State University, a post he filled from 1946 to his being named a bishop in 1959. It was the apostolate to Catholic students in secular universities that brought Tracy and Hallinan together, an apostolate where their kindred ideas and forceful leadership identified them as something of a team. Their joint efforts, along with associates such as Robert J. Welch of the University of Iowa, have been spelled out in the fine study of John Whitney Evans, *The Newman Movement. Roman Catholics in American Higher Education, 1883-1971* (Notre Dame, 1980). Bob Tracy figured prominently in the formation of the National Newman Chaplain's Association and served as the ranking officer of that group from 1954 to 1956.

It was during his tenure of that post that I first met the future bishop when he invited me to address the Newman chaplains at a Christmas Week meeting in Miami. We became good friends, and that partly because of his deep respect for history. Thus after he became the first ordinary of the new Diocese of Baton Rouge in 1961 and was making plans to attend Vatican Council II, he invited me to attend as his *peritus* since, he said, he felt an historian of the Church should be present at this extraordinary gathering. I accepted and even made a down payment on the plane fare, and then changed my mind. It was not that I was uninterested in the council, but with my limited knowledge of languages, theology, and canon law I came to the conclusion that I could better serve the Church by remaining in this country and continuing my teaching at the University of San Francisco.

Bishop Tracy might well have written me off at that point, but he remained a loyal and devoted friend, and when in September, 1965, I arrived in Rome to give a series of lectures to the students of the North American College, he sought me out and insisted that I attend the formal opening of the council's final session on September 14, which happened to be his 56th birthday. I had no real right of entry, so to speak, nor did I have with me the proper ecclesiastical garb for the occasion. In any case, the robes of a monsignor were found somewhere and I met the bishop at Saint Peter's that morning well in advance of the opening ceremony. The guards were alert to prevent 'outsiders' from getting in, but Bob instructed me to follow him as he pushed his way through the dense crowd until we arrived on the floor of the basilica. He then escorted me to the tribune overlooking the section reserved for the non-Catholic observers where I found myself in one of the lower tiers of seats several rows in front of Pedro Arrupe, General of the Jesuits, and the other generals of religious orders. It was a prime spot with a superb view of the entire *aula* and the altar where Pope Paul

VI and his attendants were celebrating the liturgy. Needless to say, I enjoyed that morning more than I can say, and I owed it entirely to the Bishop of Baton Rouge who had waved off a suspicious guard as we entered who peered closely at me looking for the pectoral cross of a bishop that was not there!

I saw Bishop Tracy several other times during those weeks in Rome, on one occasion at dinner with him and Paul Hallinan when for the first time I detected the failing health of the latter. Tracy and I corresponded from time to time in the years thereafter, and I responded as best I could to his requests for assistance relating to the book he had been asked to write on his council experience. It was published with the title *American Bishop at the Vatican Council* (New York, 1967) and an English reviewer said of it in the *Catholic Historical Review* of April, 1970:

> To all, laity and clergy, I recommend this valuable book, for it is an attractive portrayal of conciliar affairs over the period when the decrees were being hatched. There is a gentleness and sympathy about the treatment that is compelling, known in pre-conciliar times as charity. If I were asked to sum up in a phrase my reaction to this book, I would say: it is eirenic, but never ironic.

Bishop Tracy and I met a number of times after the council, at our beloved friend's funeral in Atlanta in 1968 and again in New Orleans in early October, 1969, when I was there at Archbishop Philip M. Hannan's invitation to preach at the Red Mass in the Cathedral of Saint Louis of France. Bob came down from Baton Rouge to attend the Mass and then took me to lunch at Antoine's, the famous restaurant in the French Quarter. The last decade of the life of this genial and talented prelate was overshadowed by the affliction of alcoholism which ultimately led to the resignation of his see at the age of 65. True, Bishop Tracy's declining years were darkened by this shadow, but the personal trial in no way wiped out the memory of his achievements in

Archbishop Hallinan with his friend Bishop Tracy in Saint Peter's Square during the Second Vatican Council.

behalf of the students at Louisiana State University and his decade and a half of service to his people in the Diocese of Baton Rouge.

> I am a bishop for your sake. I am a Christian together with you, a sinner together with you, a disciple and a hearer of the Gospel with you, *Vobis sum episcopus, vobiscum christianus.*[27]

I can think of no more appropriate words with which to introduce my recollections of Paul Hallinan, first Archbishop of Atlanta, than this frequently quoted expression of Saint Augustine. With the possible exception of John McNamara, there was no bishop to whom I felt closer than to this merry and rotund churchman who had been born and raised in the Diocese of Cleveland. Following his death in March, 1968, just two weeks short of his 57th birthday, I wrote two essays about the archbishop, one an article in *Thought* and the other a contribution to a volume of his writings and speeches on which I shall draw in what follows.[28]

My initial contact with Paul Hallinan came in February, 1955, when he wrote to say that he had begun work for the Ph.D. in history at Western Reserve University in Cleveland, and his major professor, Carl Wittke, had suggested that I might be helpful in the selection of a topic for the doctoral dissertation. At the time he was the Catholic chaplain at Western Reserve, having previously received his college degree at the University of Notre Dame and a master's degree at John Carroll University, along with serving

[27]Quoted by Yves Congar, O.P., "The Historical Development of Authority in the Church. Points for Christian Reflection," John M. Todd (Ed.), *Problems of Authority.* London: Darton, Longman & Todd. 1962. p. 133.

[28]"Archbishop Hallinan: In Memoriam," *Thought,* XLIII (Winter, 1968), 539-572; "A Tribute: . . . With Prudence, With Courage, With Determination," Vincent A. Yzermans (Ed.), *Days of Hope and Promise. The Writings and Speeches of Paul J. Hallinan, Archbishop of Atlanta.* Collegeville: The Liturgical Press. 1973. pp. i-xviii.

for several years as a chaplain with the armed forces during World War II. As I now recall it, we met for the first time either at the annual convention of the American Catholic Historical Association, or when I went to Cleveland to give a lecture at the Newman Club of which he was director. In any case, from that time until his death we met rather frequently and conducted a lively correspondence for a decade or more.

If I first knew the future archbishop as a graduate student in history, our acquaintance soon broadened beyond that professional bond. Everyone who knew this genial priest would, I feel sure, agree that it was exceedingly easy to establish quickly a personal relationship that was warm and open. While he had an instinctive regard for the virtue of prudence, once he had come to know and to trust a friend the latter never experienced anything suggesting the cool reserve that insecure people at times employ to keep others at a distance. The characteristic had its roots, I think, in the high premium he placed on honesty. I have rarely known any person to whom that quality seemed to come more naturally. Paul Hallinan was utterly without pretense, which is another way of saying that he was a humble man. In that regard I think of the definition of humility that my first spiritual director in the seminary, Father Francis P. Havey, S.S., gave me nearly a half century ago. The essence of humility, he said, is knowing one's place and taking it.[29]

Paul Hallinan's daily conduct was an exemplification of that principle. He had an abiding love for Cardinal Newman, and what a Newman specialist, Henry Tristram of the Birmingham Oratory, once wrote of Newman would have

[29]Hallinan would have been appalled had he read the autobiography of A.J.P. Taylor wherein the famous historian mentioned the people who got firsts in history at Oxford in his day and then commented, "I am the most distinguished and by far the best known of the lot." It was no wonder a reviewer commented, "It is perfectly true; it would still have been better left to others to say it." *Times Literary Supplement*, May 27, 1983, p. 540.

likewise been true of his American admirer. Tristram stated, "He was at once repelled by the slightest pretence or insincerity or humbug, and it was a strong condemnation from him, if he said, so and so is so unreal."[30] Doubtless it was that same love of truth and honesty that prompted Hallinan to react so favorably to my Wimmer Lecture of 1965 at Saint Vincent College which I had entitled, "A Commitment to Truth." At the time he wrote, "How essential it is to make the *honest mentality* prevail over the devious & the timid! And how discouraging it is to find the latter in high places."[31] A year and a half later he remarked in a letter, "Of everything you have done, I like *Commitment to Truth* the most."[32]

Atlanta's first archbishop was so many-sided a man that it is difficult to convey his versatility without seeming to exaggerate—or to flatter his memory which he would thoroughly deplore. I referred above to his openness of mind, and I know no better way to illustrate that trait than to say something about his attitude toward the young. I watched him mingling among the students at Cleveland where their love and respect for their Newman Club director was obvious. I do not now recall having asked myself where this priest in his mid-forties got the gift, but at least a partial answer, it seems to me, was contained in a letter written in the spring of 1964. Alluding to the prospect of Vatican Council II adopting the principle of religious freedom for all, he confessed that the subject might bring "unpleasant days ahead" due to the opposition it would arouse. He then commented:

> I think one cause is our failure to grasp the new mentality of youth. It is much more open than when I was that age, & it

[30]Henry Tristram (Ed.), *Meditations and Devotions of John Henry Newman.* New York: Longmans, Green and Company. 1953. p. xiv.

[31]Hallinan to Ellis, Atlanta, undated, received May 27, 1963.

[32]Same to same, Atlanta, July 19, 1967.

affords all the opportunities & dangers that go with openness. But must we not trust them to a high degree; & not alienate them by references to the old days, the need of prudence, caution & authority? In regard to the latter [*sic*], it seems to me that the most effective authority is that which enunciates its claim the least. I'm for 'quiet authority.'[33]

When one reflects that the archbishop translated that principle into action it is not surprising that the young found it so appealing, especially when they sensed that he in no way abandoned the need for authority in a mindless imitation of the mounting permissiveness of contemporary society.

For one who believed in and practiced 'quiet authority,' Archbishop Hallinan found a striking example of the reverse in the subject of his doctoral dissertation, Richard Gilmour, the Scottish-born Presbyterian convert who served as second Bishop of Cleveland from 1872 to his death in 1891. Very much a man of his time, Gilmour's tough disciplinary mind allowed no questioning of his authority, and were one to seek a contrast in the exercise of episcopal authority the careers of Gilmour and Hallinan would furnish an appropriate theme. Yet the latter was too good an historian to interpret Gilmour's actions in the 1880's in terms of the mentality of the 1960's. The result was a fine portrayal of the Cleveland prelate, a study that demonstrated not only thorough research set forth with literary flair, but as well an objective analysis that did not overlook Gilmour's weaknesses while crediting him with the positive achievements of his regime.

Since I devoted most of the *Thought* article of 1968 to Paul Hallinan as an historian, I shall not repeat the details here. I do wish, however, to quote a passage from a letter written just after he had successfully passed the final oral examination for the doctorate. It was typical of Hallinan's way of combining the serious with the humorous. He said:

[33]Same to same, Atlanta, May 19, 1964.

> Well—I made it! . . . the board were all most cordial; they had
> liked the dissertation & of course that helped. I filled out a
> number of papers including one questionnaire about what I
> planned to do in my 'post-doctoral' phase? Wittke & I got a
> great kick out of that!"[34]

He stated he was inviting only his family to the commencement scheduled for June 12, to which he added, "but I would
love to include you if you could possibly make it." I was due
to arrive in San Francisco several days preceding the Western Reserve event and I asked to be excused. Among a good
many decisions of my life that I later regretted this was one.
Regardless of the more than 2,000 miles between San Francisco and Cleveland I should have put off my arrival in
California or returned to honor this dear friend on one of
the great days of his life, and I felt that especially when he
was overtaken shortly thereafter by the hepatitis that caused
his untimely death.

  If one were to wish to sample the wide variety of topics to
which Archbishop Hallinan addressed himself, and that in a
way that drew increasing attention to the substantive character of these issues for both Church and State, they would
have only to note the range and depth of the 36 entries in the
Yzermans volume mentioned above. In other words, Paul
Hallinan's contribution went far beyond that of the professional historian. It is not possible here to treat the many
aspects of both civil and ecclesiastical concerns that marked
him as a discerning observer and critic who had an uncanny
ability to read 'the signs of the times' and to express their
essence in an arresting way, and that often in the face of
formidable opposition.

  For example, it was no easy task for a churchman born
and raised in the Middle West to tackle head-on the delicate
issue of racial justice in South Carolina and Georgia when
he was named Bishop of Charleston (1958) and Archbishop

[34]Hallinan to Ellis, Atlanta, undated, received May 27, 1963.

of Atlanta (1962). Yet that is precisely what he did when he made known from the outset that the Catholic communities in both areas would operate on the basis of full racial equality. In both dioceses there were Catholics who were put off by the bold initiatives of this 'northern' bishop, and yet in neither place did the policy lead to the series of ugly incidents that marked the efforts of some bishops to integrate their constituents.

Whether the generally happy outcome was due to a lack of organized opposition, to a fairly widespread acceptance of the justice of the cause, or to the prelate's tactful manner of launching the policy, it is not easy to say. In any case, he lost no time either in Charleston or in Atlanta in making his mind known. Thus on the day he was installed in Atlanta's Cathedral of Christ the King in March, 1962, he stated that it was the Catholic Church's manifest duty to champion racial justice. "Neither in the North nor in the South," he declared, "can she bear the ugly blemish of prejudice and fear," and he then added:

> Small in numbers but great in loyalty, our Catholic people are trying to reflect the unity of Christ's Mystical Body as they move toward the reality of full racial justice,—with prudence, with courage, with determination.[35]

If those were rather daring words in Georgia in 1962 they achieved the end for which they were spoken, and civil rights took another step forward with their enunciation by this extraordinarily attractive man whose endearing qualities helped to win him a hearing in both Catholic and non-Catholic circles. Nor was Hallinan's pursuit of racial justice confined to theoretical discourses as was illustrated by an episode he described for me some years later that had both its tragic and humorous aspects. He wrote:

[35]"A New Archbishop," installation sermon of Archbishop Hallinan, Cathedral of Christ the King, Atlanta, March 29, 1962, p. 37, copy.

> Just returned from an exciting evening—Mayor's Human Rel.
> Commission at the Tabernacle Baptist Church, crossed swords
> with an angry Negro preacher-cum-politician, & caused a slight
> riot when a number of the community still wanted to speak so
> when I was asked to close with prayer, I made a motion to
> continue the mtg. instead! A little after that, a rumble started
> outside (This is Boulevard Ave. where the riots were last
> summer)—a 6-year old Negro boy had been hit by a truck driver
> (white) & knocked to the street. About 70 had gathered in a foul
> mood—we got an ambulance & I drove the mother, the grand-
> mother, & 3 other little kids to the Hospital. It looked bad when
> I left after about a [*sic*] hour—hope he makes it. Of such stuff
> are riots made. (This is detailed not as a 'success story,' but to
> indicate why my correspondence is so badly neglected).[36]

Knowing the man as I did, I entertained no doubts about the
motive in which he had written; all the same, it was a 'success
story,' the like of which found frequent repetition in Paul
Hallinan's concern for others, especially for those less
favored than himself.

From Old Testament times it has been generally recognized that to certain persons there has been given the gift of
foreseeing future events and, too, of being regarded as
inspired interpreters of divine truth. I do not wish to suggest
in a simplistic way that Archbishop Hallinan was such a
person, if for no other reason that it would offend his
modesty. Yet he had an uncommon ability to put his finger
on trends and movements of his own time that proved to be
of lasting importance. For example, in the October, 1965,
debate in Vatican Council II on the Pastoral Constitution
on the Church in the Modern World, he was at pains to urge
that women's role in the Church be emphasized, declaring
that the Church had been slow, as he said, "in denouncing
the degradation of women in slavery and in claiming for
them the right of suffrage and economic equality." He then
proposed the following practical suggestions by way of
enhancing the position of women in the Church:

[36]Hallinan to Ellis, Atlanta, June 5, 1967.

That the Church define the liturgical functions of women so that they could serve as lectors and acolytes, and, when properly prepared, also, as they once did, in the apostolic office of deaconess. They could thus, as deacons do, administer certain sacraments.

That the schema should include them in the instruments to be set up after the Council to further the lay apostolate.

That women religious should have representation in those matters which concern their interests, especially in the present and post-conciliar agencies.

That every opportunity should be given to women, both as Sisters and as lay women, to offer their special talents to the ministry of the Church. Mention should also be made of women who are not married. Because of the universal call of women (in *De Ecclesia*), they also promote family values by witnessing in their own way to this universal vocation.[37]

Nor did he rest the case there. A year later in an address that showed he had been keeping abreast of the movement with reference to Betty Friedan, Barbara Streisand *et al.*, he once again championed women's rights within the Church with his customary verve.[38]

Another instance of the archbishop's vision was the pastoral letter on war and peace that he issued in October, 1966, with his auxiliary bishop, Joseph L. Bernardin, the present Cardinal Archbishop of Chicago. True, this letter did not touch all the aspects of the American bishops' detailed pastoral letter of May, 1983. But that it did anticipate by 16 years some of the most controversial features of that famous document was evident from the questions which the Atlanta bishops raised when they wrote:

As the great debate on war and peace gathers momentum, certain urgent questions demand that we respond:
1. What are the demands of true patriotism?

[37]Written intervention, October 12, 1965, Yzermans, *American Participation in the Second Vatican Council*, p. 202.

[38]"Wanted: Valiant Women," address to the Archdiocesan Council of Catholic Women, Omaha, Nebraska, September 20, 1966, Yzermans, *Days of Hope and Promise*, pp. 135-141.

2. Is it possible to speak of a just war today as we did in the past?
3. On a broader level, should nations try to maintain peace by a balance of terror?
4. Does universal disarmament (all sides) differ morally from unilateral disarmament (one side)?
5. What are our obligations in contributing toward a genuinely moral consensus regarding American involvement in Viet Nam?[39]

If I have headed my remarks about the late Archbishop of Atlanta *'facile princeps,'* it is because I regard him as the most striking example of episcopal leadership in the American Catholic community of my time. Definitions of what constitutes leadership abound, and I do not flatter myself that I can add anything of significance on that score. All things considered, I have found Norman Cousins' explanation a satisfactory one. He stated:

> What is the function of leadership? There would be little difficulty in obtaining general agreement on the proposition that the job of leaders is to convert large problems into opportunities, to inspire people to meet difficult challenges, and to brood creatively about purpose.[40]

Paul Hallinan personified these traits in his promotion of racial justice, of women's rights, and in raising anguished questions concerning the threat of nuclear warfare. In these matters he furnished imaginative leadership that was at once provocative and constructive, and that not only to his fellow Catholics but to the nation at large. It was a service he rendered on a world scale by his forceful and persistent efforts in behalf of a reform of the Church's liturgy both during and after Vatican Council II. In so doing he became an exemplar of the qualities of leadership featured by *Time*

[39]"War and Peace. A Pastoral Letter to the Archdiocese of Atlanta, October, 1966," John Tracy Ellis (Ed.), *Documents of American Catholic History.* Revised and enlarged edition. Chicago: Henry Regnery Company. 1967. II, 698.

[40]"Thinking Through Leadership," *Saturday Review/World,* November 16, 1974, p. 4.

magazine in its special issues on that topic (July 15, 1974; November 8, 1976; August 6, 1979). And in saying this there is no implied denial of the contributions made by Hallinan's fellow Americans in the conciliar debates.

The Catholic community of the United States that Paul Hallinan left 15 years ago still bears the scars that were inflicted during his last decade in this world. The causes for this deep malaise are many and varied, but I wonder if the most serious is not the pervasive divisiveness that has set Catholic against Catholic in an internecine strife that has invaded virtually every diocese, parish, and community of religious men and women in the land. And among the subjects on which they differ none, it seems to me, has engendered more bitterness, ironically, than the liturgy.

Of the many aspects of religious life with which Archbishop Hallinan was identified, I suspect that historically his name will be more closely linked to liturgical reform than to any other single topic, the evidence of which was gathered and published in the works of Vincent A. Yzermans to which I have made reference here. Vatican Council II was not 3 weeks old when Hallinan rose to the podium in Saint Peter's to declare:

> I speak for many bishops (although not for all) of the United States of America who hope for the more vital, conscious and fruitful participation of our people in the Mass... The liturgy of the Church must be public, but this can have real meaning for our people only if they understand enough of it to be a part of it.

Then with an eye to the effect the suggested changes might have on Christians outside the Church of Rome, he added, "The more we can do to render the Mass understandable to all, not just to those equipped by learning or formed by habit, the more we open new avenues to the minds and hearts of Christians who are not Catholic."[41]

[41]Yzermans, *American Participation in the Second Vatican Council*, p. 157.

It was a battle he waged with relentless energy against the conservative bishops up to the December day in 1963 when the constitution on the liturgy was finally promulgated by Pope Paul VI. Nor did Hallinan relax his efforts during the post-conciliar years. One of the things for which he worked was the establishment of centers of liturgical experimentation, a request that Rome initially denied. Three weeks before he died he telephoned me in San Francisco early one morning and we talked for almost an hour. I sensed that this was his 'good-by,' for he realized that the end was near. I alluded to the Roman denial, but that the dying archbishop had meanwhile lost none of his conviction on the issue was evident when the weakened voice from far-off Atlanta was heard to say, "We'll go back again, John, we'll go back again." It is pleasant to recall that later his fellow bishops did 'go back again' and won the permission that had at first been refused, and it is still more pleasant to think that their persistence may well have been strengthened by the dogged determination of their recently deceased brother of Atlanta.

When word reached me in San Francisco that my friend had died I felt I owed it to his memory to attend the funeral. In that springtime of late March, 1968, Atlanta was aglow with the blossoming dogwood on all sides. The cathedral in which he had been installed as archbishop only 6 years before was filled to capacity, with his brother and his family heading the large gathering that had come from distant places to bid farewell to one who had made so deep an impression on their lives. I recall meeting the auxiliary bishop, Joseph Bernardin, at the side of the cathedral before the Mass began when we exchanged a few recollections of our departed friend that brought tears to the eyes of both of us. Yet in the spirit of the new liturgy that Archbishop Hallinan had worked so hard to implement there was a note of joy mingled with the sadness of the occasion. Rarely in my life have I felt the death of a friend with the keenness that I did in the case of Paul Hallinan. As I flew back to San

Francisco that afternoon there passed through my mind memories of our many happy meetings and our extensive correspondence. More important, however, was the memory of the example of his life by which I and so many others had been enriched. If his being taken at the age of 57 left one pondering the mystery of it all, the sense of loss was mitigated by the knowledge of his own reconciliation to God's will. True, his years had been relatively few, but they had been genuinely fruitful ones that fulfilled what the psalmist had in mind when he wrote, "Man goes forth to his work, to labor till evening falls."[42]

As I come to the close of this memoir I am conscious of having omitted other churchmen whom I knew before they became bishops, but with whom I had little or no contact after their change of status. Francis J. Haas (1889-1953) was such a person, for although we taught at the same university from 1935 to 1943 when he was named Bishop of Grand Rapids, I could not say that I knew him at all well. The same was true of others who appeared on the university campus from time to time such as Cardinals Dennis Dougherty of Philadelphia, Patrick Hayes of New York, and Albert Meyer of Chicago, whom I knew by sight but scarcely more than to be familiar with stories that circulated about them in clerical circles.

While I have made a conscious effort to be objective in what I have written here, I am not so foolish as to believe that I have succeeded to a perfect degree. The autobiographer like the historian cannot entirely divest his or herself of their prejudices and preferences, but they must at least make a constant and serious attempt to achieve that goal. In that regard the autobiographer operates under a special kind of threat that was described some time ago by a psychotherapist as "an inbuilt tendency towards something

---

[42]*Psalm* 104.

that has, I think, to be called falsification." He explained what he meant in this way:

> The process of detaching that thread which is one's own life from the fabric which has been simultaneously woven by those around one, introduces an inherent bias towards egocentricity, at the expense of objectivity, and towards exaggeration of one's difference and alienation from others.[43]

I readily admit the 'difference' from those about whom I have written, but I think the 'alienation' from them has been less marked. In the final analysis, however, the judgment of my success or failure must be left to those who read this memoir. Allowing for the more exalted character of the sources with which the Scripture scholar deals, the autobiographer who is a believer may, I hope, share to some degree in the ideal and approach described in the book of Sirach when the ancient writer declared:

> The man who devotes himself
>   to the study of the law of the Most High
> Explores the wisdom of the men of old
>   and occupies himself with the prophecies;
> He treasures the discourses of famous men,
>   and goes to the heart of involved sayings;
> He studies obscure parables,
>   and is busied with the hidden meanings of the sages.[44]

[43]Charles Rycroft, "Viewpoint: Analysis and the Autobiographer," *Times Literary Supplement*, May 27, 1983. p. 541.

[44]Sirach, 39: 1-3.

INDEX

179